THE AUSTRALIAN
Women's Weekly
bakes & gratins

acp
books

Contents

The oven temperatures in this book are for conventional ovens; if you have a fan-forced oven, decrease the temperature by 10-20 degrees.

pasta

carbonara gnocchi bake

1 tablespoon olive oil
1 medium brown onion (150g), chopped finely
3 cloves garlic, crushed
4 rindless bacon slices (260g), chopped coarsely
1½ cups (375ml) pouring cream
500g (1 pound) potato gnocchi
2 egg yolks
⅔ cup (50g) finely grated parmesan cheese
½ cup (35g) stale coarse breadcrumbs

1 Preheat oven to 200°C/400°F. Oil deep 1.5-litre (6-cup) ovenproof dish.
2 Heat oil in large frying pan; cook onion, garlic and bacon, stirring, until onion softens and bacon is crisp. Add cream; simmer, uncovered, about 5 minutes or until sauce thickens slightly. Season to taste. Cool.
3 Meanwhile, cook gnocchi in large saucepan of boiling water until tender; drain.
4 Combine gnocchi, sauce, egg yolks and half the cheese in large bowl; pour mixture into dish. Sprinkle with combined remaining cheese and breadcrumbs. Cover dish with foil; bake 25 minutes. Uncover; bake about 15 minutes or until browned.

prep + cook time 55 minutes **serves** 4
nutritional count per serving 59.2g total fat (33.2g saturated fat); 3511kJ (840 cal); 47.3g carbohydrate; 28.6g protein; 4.3g fibre

serving suggestion Serve with crusty bread and a leafy green salad.

chicken and broad bean rigatoni bake

500g (1 pound) frozen broad beans (fava beans)
2 cups (500ml) salt-reduced chicken stock
400g (12½ ounces) chicken breast fillets
375g (12 ounces) rigatoni pasta
60g (2 ounces) butter
⅓ cup (50g) plain (all-purpose) flour
1 cup (250ml) milk
2 teaspoons finely grated lemon rind
½ cup (40g) finely grated parmesan cheese
½ cup (65g) finely chopped roasted
  unsalted pistachios
½ cup (35g) stale breadcrumbs

1 Boil, steam or microwave beans until tender; drain, peel away grey skins.
2 Bring stock to the boil in medium saucepan. Add chicken; simmer, covered, 10 minutes. Cool chicken in poaching liquid 10 minutes. Drain chicken, reserve liquid; shred chicken coarsely.
3 Preheat oven to 200°C/400°F. Oil 2.5-litre (10-cup) ovenproof dish.
4 Cook pasta in large saucepan of boiling water until tender; drain.
5 Meanwhile, melt butter in large saucepan. Add flour; cook, stirring, about 2 minutes or until mixture bubbles and thickens. Gradually stir in combined milk and reserved liquid. Cook, stirring, until sauce boils and thickens.
6 Stir pasta, chicken, beans, rind and half the cheese into pan; season to taste. Spread mixture into dish; sprinkle with combined remaining cheese, nuts and breadcrumbs. Bake, uncovered, about 20 minutes or until browned.

prep + cook time 55 minutes serves 6
nutritional count per serving 22.6g total fat
(10g saturated fat); 2378kJ (569 cal);
57.8g carbohydrate; 31.2g protein; 4.8g fibre

seafood mornay lasagnes

6 lasagne sheets (170g)
60g (2 ounces) butter
⅓ cup (50g) plain (all-purpose) flour
2 cups (500ml) milk
½ cup (125ml) dry white wine
2 teaspoons finely grated lemon rind
¼ cup finely chopped fresh flat-leaf parsley
200g (6½ ounces) uncooked medium
  king prawns (shrimp)
200g (6½ ounces) firm white fish fillets
250g (8½ ounces) crab meat
½ cup (40g) finely grated parmesan cheese

1 Preheat oven to 220°C/425°F. Oil six 1¼-cup
(310ml) ovenproof dishes.
2 Cook lasagne sheets, in batches, in large
saucepan of boiling water until tender; drain.
Cut each sheet into three squares.
3 Meanwhile, melt butter in large saucepan.
Add flour; cook, stirring, about 2 minutes or until
mixture bubbles and thickens. Gradually stir in
milk and wine. Cook, stirring, until sauce boils
and thickens; cool. Stir in rind and parsley; season
to taste.
4 Shell and devein prawns; cut prawns and
fish into 1cm (½-inch) pieces. Combine prawns,
fish and crab in medium bowl.
5 Line base of each dish with one piece of
lasagne. Top each with half the seafood, one-third
of the sauce, then another piece of lasagne. Top
each with remaining seafood, half the remaining
sauce and another lasagne sheet. Top each with
remaining sauce; sprinkle with cheese. Bake about
15 minutes or until seafood is cooked.

prep + cook time 45 minutes **serves** 6
nutritional count per serving 15.1g total fat
(9.3g saturated fat); 1555kJ (372 cal);
30.6g carbohydrate; 25.1g protein; 1.4g fibre

tip Use fresh, instant or dried lasagne for
this recipe.
note We used larger dishes here – each will
serve three.

rocket pesto and spaghetti frittata

200g (6½ ounces) spaghetti
250g (8 ounces) rocket (arugula),
  chopped coarsely
2 tablespoons roasted pine nuts
¼ cup (20g) finely grated parmesan cheese
2 teaspoons finely grated lemon rind
2 cloves garlic, quartered
2 tablespoons olive oil
⅓ cup (50g) semi-dried tomatoes in oil,
  drained, chopped finely
6 eggs
1 cup (250ml) pouring cream

1 Preheat oven to 200°C/400°F. Oil deep 19cm
(7½-inch) square cake pan; line base and sides
with baking paper, extending paper 5cm (2 inches)
over sides. Or, oil deep ovenproof frying pan with
base measuring 20cm (8 inches).
2 Cook pasta in large saucepan of boiling water
until tender; drain.
3 Meanwhile, blend or process rocket, nuts,
cheese, rind, garlic and oil until pesto is smooth.
4 Combine pasta, pesto and tomato in large bowl;
season to taste. Spread mixture into pan. Whisk
eggs and cream in large jug until combined; pour
over pasta mixture. Bake frittata, uncovered,
about 35 minutes or until set. Stand frittata in
pan 5 minutes before cutting.

prep + cook time 55 minutes **serves** 6
nutritional count per serving 35.1g total fat
(15.4g saturated fat); 2057kJ (492 cal);
28.2g carbohydrate; 15.1g protein; 3.4g fibre

serving suggestion Serve with a garden salad.

spaghetti rosa bake

250g (8 ounces) spaghetti
1 tablespoon olive oil
1 medium brown onion (150g), chopped finely
2 cloves garlic, crushed
2⅔ cups (700g) bottled tomato pasta sauce
2 tablespoons finely chopped fresh basil
½ cup (125ml) pouring cream
1½ cups (150g) coarsely grated mozzarella cheese

1 Preheat oven to 200°C/400°F. Oil shallow 2-litre (8-cup) ovenproof dish.
2 Cook pasta in large saucepan of boiling water until tender; drain.
3 Meanwhile, heat oil in large saucepan; cook onion and garlic, stirring, until onion softens. Add sauce and basil; bring to the boil. Reduce heat; simmer, uncovered, about 10 minutes or until sauce is thickened slightly. Stir in cream; season.
4 Stir pasta and half the cheese into hot sauce in pan; spread mixture into dish. Sprinkle with remaining cheese. Bake about 20 minutes or until browned lightly.

prep + cook time 40 minutes **serves** 6
nutritional count per serving 19.9g total fat (10.1g saturated fat); 1668kJ (399 cal); 39.4g carbohydrate; 13.9g protein; 4.5g fibre

penne arrabbiata bake

300g (9½ ounces) penne pasta
1 tablespoon olive oil
1 medium brown onion (150g), chopped finely
3 cloves garlic, crushed
1 fresh long red chilli, chopped finely
6 drained anchovy fillets, chopped finely
2 tablespoons finely chopped fresh basil
2⅔ cups (700g) bottled tomato pasta sauce
½ cup (60g) seeded black olives,
  chopped coarsely
½ cup (55g) pizza cheese

1 Preheat oven to 180°C/350°F. Oil deep 2-litre (8-cup) ovenproof dish.
2 Cook pasta in large saucepan of boiling water until tender; drain.
3 Meanwhile, heat oil in large saucepan; cook onion, garlic, chilli, anchovy and basil, stirring, until onion softens. Add sauce; bring to the boil. Remove from heat; stir pasta and olives into hot sauce. Season to taste.
4 Spoon mixture into dish; sprinkle with cheese. Bake about 25 minutes or until browned lightly.

prep + cook time 45 minutes serves 4
nutritional count per serving 12g total fat
(3.1g saturated fat); 1977kJ (473 cal);
70.1g carbohydrate; 17.5g protein; 7.5g fibre

This recipe uses four lasagne sheets but only has three pasta layers. We used the fourth sheet to trim and fill any gaps in each pasta layer.

tomato, beef and pea lasagne

1 tablespoon olive oil
1 medium brown onion (150g), chopped finely
2 cloves garlic, crushed
500g (1 pound) minced (ground) beef
800g (1½ pounds) canned diced tomatoes
½ cup (125ml) beef stock
¼ cup (70g) tomato paste
2 tablespoons finely chopped fresh basil
1 cup (120g) frozen peas
60g (2 ounces) butter
⅓ cup (50g) plain (all-purpose) flour
3 cups (750ml) hot milk
1½ cups (150g) pizza cheese
4 fresh lasagne sheets

1 Heat oil in large frying pan; cook onion and garlic, stirring, until onion softens. Add beef; cook, stirring, until browned. Add undrained tomatoes, stock, paste and basil; bring to the boil. Reduce heat; simmer, covered, 30 minutes. Uncover; simmer, about 10 minutes or until sauce thickens slightly. Stir in peas; season to taste.
2 Meanwhile, melt butter in large saucepan. Add flour; cook, stirring, about 2 minutes or until mixture bubbles and thickens. Gradually stir in milk; cook, stirring, until sauce boils and thickens. Remove from heat; stir in half the cheese.
3 Preheat oven to 200°C/400°F. Oil deep 3.5-litre (14-cup) ovenproof dish.
4 Line base of dish with lasagne sheets, trimming to fit. Top with half the beef mixture, one-third of the cheese sauce, then more lasagne sheets, trimming to fit. Top with remaining beef mixture, half the remaining cheese sauce and remaining lasagne sheets, trimming to fit. Top with remaining cheese sauce; sprinkle with remaining cheese.
5 Cover lasagne with foil; bake 35 minutes. Uncover; bake about 20 minutes or until browned lightly. Stand lasagne 10 minutes before serving.

prep + cook time 1½ hours **serves** 8
nutritional count per serving 19.2g total fat (11.5g saturated fat); 1530kJ (366 cal); 22g carbohydrate; 25.3g protein; 3.6g fibre

asparagus, egg and bacon bake

250g (8 ounces) penne pasta
1 tablespoon olive oil
1 medium brown onion (150g), chopped finely
3 cloves garlic, crushed
3 rindless bacon slices (195g), sliced thinly
300g (9½ ounces) asparagus, trimmed,
  chopped coarsely
2 tablespoons plain (all-purpose) flour
½ cup (125ml) dry white wine
½ cup (125ml) chicken stock
1 cup (250ml) pouring cream
4 hard-boiled eggs, quartered
2 tablespoons finely chopped fresh chives
1 cup (80g) finely grated parmesan cheese
⅓ cup (25g) stale breadcrumbs

1 Preheat oven to 220°C/425°F. Oil deep 2.5-litre
(10-cup) ovenproof dish.
2 Cook pasta in large saucepan of boiling water
until tender; drain.
3 Meanwhile, heat oil in large saucepan; cook
onion, garlic and bacon, stirring, until bacon is
crisp. Add asparagus; cook, stirring, until tender.
Add flour; cook, stirring, about 2 minutes or until
mixture bubbles and thickens. Gradually stir in
wine, stock and cream. Cook, stirring, until mixture
boils and thickens.
4 Stir pasta, eggs, chives and half the cheese
into asparagus mixture; season to taste.
Spoon mixture into dish; sprinkle with combined
remaining cheese and breadcrumbs. Bake about
20 minutes or until browned lightly.

prep + cook time 45 minutes **serves** 6
nutritional count per serving 32.6g total fat
(17.4g saturated fat); 2345kJ (561 cal);
37.8g carbohydrate; 24.6g protein; 3.1g fibre

pumpkin, spinach and ricotta cannelloni

400g (12½ ounces) pumpkin, chopped coarsely
200g (6½ ounces) frozen spinach, thawed
200g (6½ ounces) ricotta cheese
12 cannelloni tubes (150g)
2⅔ cups (700g) bottled tomato pasta sauce
½ cup (60g) coarsely grated cheddar cheese
½ cup (40g) finely grated parmesan cheese

1 Preheat oven to 200°C/400°F. Oil shallow
1.5-litre (6-cup) ovenproof dish.
2 Boil, steam or microwave pumpkin until
tender; drain. Mash pumpkin in medium bowl
until smooth; cool.
3 Squeeze excess liquid from spinach; chop
coarsely. Stir spinach and ricotta into pumpkin;
season to taste. Fill cannelloni tubes with
pumpkin mixture.
4 Spread half the sauce over base of dish;
top with cannelloni, in single layer. Pour remaining
sauce over cannelloni; sprinkle with combined
cheddar and parmesan.
5 Cover dish with foil; bake 35 minutes. Uncover;
bake about 20 minutes or until cannelloni are
tender and cheese is browned lightly.

prep + cook time 1 hour 20 minutes **serves** 4
nutritional count per serving 17.8g total fat
(9.5g saturated fat); 1910kJ (457 cal);
46.3g carbohydrate; 23.7g protein; 9g fibre

serving suggestion Serve with a leafy green salad.
tip We used butternut pumpkin for this recipe.

spinach and ricotta pasta slice

300g (9½ ounces) angel hair pasta
410g (13 ounces) canned tomato puree
150g (4½ ounces) baby spinach leaves
300g (9½ ounces) ricotta cheese
4 eggs
½ cup (125ml) pouring cream
½ cup (55g) pizza cheese

1 Preheat oven to 200°C/400°F. Oil shallow 2-litre (8-cup) ovenproof dish.
2 Cook pasta in large saucepan of boiling water until tender; drain, cool.
3 Spread one-third of the tomato puree over base of dish; top with half the spinach, half the pasta and half the ricotta. Pour half the remaining tomato puree over ricotta; top with remaining spinach and remaining pasta. Pour remaining tomato puree over pasta; sprinkle with remaining ricotta.
4 Whisk eggs and cream in large jug until combined; season. Pour egg mixture over pasta; sprinkle with pizza cheese. Bake, uncovered, about 40 minutes or until browned lightly and set.

prep + cook time 1 hour serves 6
nutritional count per serving 20.9g total fat (12g saturated fat); 1802kJ (431 cal); 39.1g carbohydrate; 19.9g protein; 3.6g fibre

broccoli and cheese penne with garlic and lemon crumbs

200g (6½ ounces) penne pasta
500g (1 pound) broccoli, cut into small florets
3 eggs
1 cup (250ml) pouring cream
⅓ cup (80ml) milk
⅔ cup (80g) coarsely grated cheddar cheese
½ cup (35g) stale breadcrumbs
1 cup (80g) finely grated parmesan cheese
2 cloves garlic, crushed
1 tablespoon finely grated lemon rind
2 tablespoons finely chopped fresh
  flat-leaf parsley

1 Preheat oven to 220°C/425°F. Oil deep 2-litre (8-cup) ovenproof dish.
2 Cook pasta in large saucepan of boiling water until tender. Add broccoli for last 5 minutes of pasta cooking time; drain. Rinse pasta and broccoli under cold water; drain, cool.
3 Combine pasta, broccoli, eggs, cream, milk and cheddar in large bowl; season. Spoon mixture into dish; sprinkle with combined breadcrumbs, parmesan, garlic, rind and parsley. Bake, uncovered, about 40 minutes or until browned lightly and set. Stand 10 minutes before serving.

prep + cook time 1 hour serves 6
nutritional count per serving 30.5g total fat
(18.8g saturated fat); 2048kJ (490 cal);
29.3g carbohydrate; 21.6g protein; 5.1g fibre

17

pastitsio

1 tablespoon olive oil
1 medium brown onion (150g), chopped finely
2 cloves garlic, crushed
500g (1 pound) minced (ground) beef
1 teaspoon ground cinnamon
½ teaspoon ground nutmeg
800g (1½ pounds) canned diced tomatoes
½ cup (125ml) dry white wine
½ cup (125ml) beef stock
¼ cup (70g) tomato paste
2 tablespoons finely chopped fresh
   flat-leaf parsley
200g (6½ ounces) macaroni pasta
1 egg
1 cup (80g) finely grated parmesan cheese
¼ cup (15g) stale breadcrumbs

CHEESE TOPPING
60g (2 ounces) butter
⅓ cup (50g) plain (all-purpose) flour
2 cups (500ml) hot milk
1 cup (80g) finely grated parmesan cheese
1 egg yolk

1 Heat oil in large frying pan; cook onion and garlic, stirring, until onion softens. Add beef and spices; cook, stirring, until browned and fragrant. Add undrained tomatoes, wine, stock and paste; bring to the boil. Reduce heat; simmer, covered, 30 minutes. Uncover; simmer, about 5 minutes or until sauce thickens slightly. Stir in parsley; season to taste.
2 Meanwhile, make cheese topping.
3 Preheat oven to 200°C/400°F. Oil shallow 2-litre (8-cup) ovenproof dish.
4 Cook pasta in large saucepan of boiling water until tender; drain. Combine pasta and egg in large bowl. Spoon pasta mixture into dish; top with beef mixture. Spread cheese topping over beef mixture; sprinkle with combined cheese and breadcrumbs. Bake, uncovered, about 25 minutes or until browned lightly. Stand 5 minutes before serving.

CHEESE TOPPING Melt butter in medium saucepan. Add flour; cook, stirring, about 2 minutes or until mixture bubbles and thickens. Gradually stir in milk; cook, stirring, until sauce boils and thickens. Remove from heat; stir in cheese and egg yolk.

prep + cook time 1½ hours serves 6
nutritional count per serving 32.2g total fat (17.3g saturated fat); 2638kJ (631 cal); 41.7g carbohydrate; 38.4g protein; 4.2g fibre

classic macaroni cheese

375g (12 ounces) macaroni pasta
60g (2 ounces) butter
¼ cup (35g) plain (all-purpose) flour
3 cups (750ml) hot milk
1½ cups (180g) coarsely grated cheddar cheese
1 cup (70g) stale coarse white breadcrumbs

1 Preheat oven to 180°C/350°F. Oil 1.5-litre (6-cup) ovenproof dish.
2 Cook pasta in large saucepan of boiling water until tender; drain.

3 Meanwhile, melt butter in large saucepan. Add flour; cook, stirring, about 2 minutes or until mixture bubbles and thickens. Gradually stir in milk. Cook, stirring, until sauce boils and thickens. Stir in 1 cup (120g) of the cheese.
4 Stir pasta into hot sauce mixture; spoon into dish. Sprinkle with combined breadcrumbs and remaining cheese. Bake, uncovered, about 25 minutes or until browned lightly.

prep + cook time 1 hour **serves** 4
nutritional count per serving 36.5g total fat (22.9g saturated fat); 3432kJ (821 cal); 89.7g carbohydrate; 31.5g protein; 4.1g fibre

tip we used ciabatta to make the breadcrumbs.

tuna mornay with pasta

375g (12 ounces) elbow pasta
60g (2 ounces) butter
1 medium brown onion (150g), chopped finely
1 clove garlic, crushed
2 stalks celery (300g), trimmed, chopped finely
¼ cup (35g) plain (all-purpose) flour
1½ cups (375ml) hot milk
1 cup (250ml) pouring cream
425g (13½ ounces) canned tuna in springwater,
  drained, flaked
2 tablespoons finely chopped fresh
  flat-leaf parsley
2 teaspoons finely grated lemon rind
1 cup (70g) stale coarse breadcrumbs
1 cup (120g) coarsely grated cheddar cheese

1 Preheat oven to 180°C/350°F. Oil deep 2.5-litre (10-cup) ovenproof dish.
2 Cook pasta in large saucepan of boiling water until tender; drain.
3 Melt butter in large saucepan; cook onion, garlic and celery, stirring, until onion softens. Add flour; cook, stirring, about 2 minutes or until mixture bubbles and thickens. Gradually stir in milk and cream. Cook, stirring, until sauce boils and thickens.
4 Stir pasta, tuna, parsley and rind into sauce mixture; season. Spoon mixture into dish; sprinkle with combined breadcrumbs and cheese. Bake, uncovered, about 35 minutes or until browned lightly.

prep + cook time 1 hour **serves** 6
nutritional count per serving 38g total fat (24g saturated fat); 2997kJ (717 cal); 61.1g carbohydrate; 31g protein; 3.8g fibre

creamy bolognese pasta bake

1 tablespoon olive oil
1 medium brown onion (150g), chopped finely
3 cloves garlic, crushed
2 stalks celery (300g), trimmed, chopped finely
1 large carrot (180g), chopped finely
500g (1 pound) minced (ground) beef
½ cup (125ml) dry red wine
½ cup (125ml) beef stock
410g (13 ounces) canned diced tomatoes
⅓ cup (95g) tomato paste
1 cup (250ml) milk
½ cup (60g) frozen peas
¼ cup finely chopped fresh flat-leaf parsley
300g (9½ ounces) rigatoni pasta
1½ cups (180g) coarsely grated cheddar cheese

1 Heat oil in large saucepan; cook onion, garlic, celery and carrot, stirring, until vegetables soften. Add beef; cook, stirring, until browned. Add wine; bring to the boil. Boil, uncovered, until liquid is almost evaporated. Add stock, undrained tomatoes, paste and milk; bring to the boil. Reduce heat; simmer, uncovered, about 30 minutes or until sauce thickens slightly. Stir in peas and parsley; season to taste.
2 Preheat oven to 220°C/425°F. Oil deep 3-litre (12-cup) ovenproof dish.
3 Cook pasta in large saucepan of boiling water until tender; drain.
4 Stir pasta into bolognese mixture with half the cheese. Spoon mixture into dish; sprinkle with remaining cheese. Bake, uncovered, about 15 minutes or until browned lightly. Stand 5 minutes before serving.

prep + cook time 1 hour 10 minutes serves 6
nutritional count per serving 22g total fat
(11.2g saturated fat); 2245kJ (537 cal);
44.2g carbohydrate; 34g protein; 5.8g fibre

vegetables

eggplant parmigiana

2 medium eggplants (600g)
2 teaspoons coarse cooking (kosher) salt
1 tablespoon olive oil
1 medium brown onion (150g), chopped finely
2 cloves garlic, crushed
2 tablespoons finely chopped fresh basil
2⅔ cups (700g) bottled tomato pasta sauce
1½ cups (150g) coarsely grated mozzarella cheese
½ cup (40g) finely grated parmesan cheese
½ cup (35g) stale coarse breadcrumbs

1 Peel and discard strips of skin from eggplant; cut eggplant into 5mm (¼-inch) slices. Place eggplant in colander; sprinkle with salt. Stand in sink 30 minutes. Rinse eggplant under cold water; drain. Squeeze excess water from eggplant.
2 Meanwhile, heat oil in medium saucepan; cook onion, garlic and basil, stirring, until onion softens. Add sauce; bring to the boil. Reduce heat; simmer, uncovered, about 15 minutes or until sauce thickens slightly. Season to taste.
3 Preheat oven to 220°C/425°F. Oil six 1¼-cup (310ml) ovenproof dishes.
4 Spoon half the sauce into dishes; top with half the eggplant and half the mozzarella. Top with remaining eggplant, remaining sauce, then remaining mozzarella. Sprinkle with combined parmesan and breadcrumbs.
5 Cover dishes with foil; place on oven tray. Bake about 40 minutes or until eggplant is tender. Uncover; bake about 15 minutes or until browned lightly.

prep + cook time 1 hour 15 minutes **serves** 6
nutritional count per serving 13.2g total fat (5.5g saturated fat); 1041kJ (249 cal); 16.9g carbohydrate; 13.4g protein; 5.6g fibre

note We've used larger dishes here – each dish will serve three.

spinach and kumara gnocchi

1kg (2 pounds) kumara (orange sweet potato),
  chopped coarsely
2 medium potatoes (400g), chopped coarsely
½ cup finely chopped spinach leaves
1 cup (150g) plain (all-purpose)
  flour, approximately
½ cup (40g) finely grated parmesan cheese

TOMATO BASIL SAUCE
1 tablespoon olive oil
1 small brown onion (80g), chopped finely
2 cloves garlic, crushed
4 medium tomatoes (600g), chopped finely
¼ cup finely chopped fresh basil

1 Preheat oven to 200°C/400°F. Oil six shallow 1½-cup (375ml) ovenproof dishes.
2 Roast kumara and potato, in single layer, on oiled oven tray, about 40 minutes or until tender; cool.
3 Meanwhile, make tomato basil sauce.
4 Push kumara and potato through potato ricer or sieve into large bowl. Stir in spinach and enough of the sifted flour to make a soft, sticky dough.
5 To make gnocchi flatten dough on floured surface to 1cm (½-inch) thickness. Cut 5cm (2-inch) rounds from dough; transfer gnocchi to tea-towel-lined tray. Reshape and cut rounds from any remaining dough until all dough is used.
6 Cook gnocchi, in batches, in large saucepan of boiling water until gnocchi float to the surface and are cooked through. Remove gnocchi using slotted spoon; transfer to dishes. Top with sauce, sprinkle with cheese. Bake, uncovered, about 15 minutes or until browned lightly.

TOMATO BASIL SAUCE Heat oil in medium saucepan; cook onion and garlic, stirring, until onion softens. Add tomato; cook, stirring, about 5 minutes or until tomato softens. Simmer, uncovered, 10 minutes or until sauce thickens slightly. Stir in basil; season to taste.

prep + cook time 1½ hours serves 6
nutritional count per serving 5.8g total fat (1.9g saturated fat); 1233kJ (295 cal); 46.6g carbohydrate; 10.4g protein; 5.9g fibre

tip You will need to buy one bunch of spinach (300g/9½ ounces) to make this recipe.

curried lentil pies

2 tablespoons ghee
1 medium brown onion (150g), chopped finely
2 cloves garlic, crushed
4cm (1½-inch) piece fresh ginger (20g), grated
1 fresh long red chilli, chopped finely
1 stalk celery (150g), chopped coarsely
1 large carrot (180g), chopped coarsely
2 teaspoons each black mustard seeds, ground
  cumin and ground coriander
1 teaspoon ground turmeric
1½ cups (300g) brown lentils
410g (13 ounces) canned crushed tomatoes
2 cups (500ml) vegetable stock
⅔ cup (160ml) coconut milk
½ cup (60g) frozen peas
½ cup coarsely chopped fresh coriander (cilantro)
600g (1¼ pounds) pumpkin, chopped coarsely
2 medium potatoes (400g), chopped coarsely
60g (2 ounces) butter

1 Heat ghee in large saucepan; cook onion, garlic, ginger, chilli, celery and carrot, stirring, until vegetables soften. Add spices; cook, stirring, until fragrant. Add lentils, undrained tomatoes and stock; simmer, covered, stirring occasionally, about 1 hour or until lentils are tender. Stir in coconut milk, peas and coriander; season to taste.
2 Meanwhile, boil, steam or microwave pumpkin and potato until tender; drain. Mash pumpkin and potato with butter in medium bowl until smooth.
3 Preheat oven to 220°C/425°F. Oil four deep 1¼-cup (310ml) ovenproof dishes.
4 Divide lentil mixture among dishes; top with pumpkin mixture. Bake, uncovered, about 20 minutes or until browned lightly. Sprinkle with black sesame seeds if you like.

prep + cook time 1 hour serves 4
nutritional count per serving 31.9g total fat (21.7g saturated fat); 2796kJ (669 cal); 60.3g carbohydrate; 28.3g protein; 18.9g fibre

vegie casserole with chive dumplings

1 tablespoon olive oil
1 large leek (500g), sliced thinly
2 cloves garlic, crushed
3 rindless bacon slices (195g), chopped coarsely
2 stalks celery (300g), trimmed, chopped coarsely
1 large carrot (180g), chopped coarsely
2 medium red capsicums (bell peppers) (400g),
  chopped coarsely
2 medium zucchini (240g), chopped coarsely
½ cup (125ml) dry red wine
410g (13 ounces) canned crushed tomatoes
1 cup (250ml) water
400g (12½ ounces) swiss brown
  mushrooms, halved
½ cup (60g) frozen peas

CHIVE DUMPLINGS
1½ cups (225g) self-raising flour
60g (2 ounces) butter, chopped finely
¾ cup (60g) finely grated parmesan cheese
2 tablespoons finely chopped fresh chives
½ cup (125ml) milk, approximately

1 Preheat oven to 180°C/350°F.
2 Heat oil in large flameproof casserole dish; cook
leek, garlic and bacon, stirring, until leek softens
and bacon is crisp. Add celery, carrot, capsicum,
zucchini, wine, undrained tomatoes and the water;
bring to the boil. Cover; bake about 20 minutes
or until vegetables are tender.
3 Meanwhile, make chive dumplings.
4 Remove dish from oven; stir in mushrooms
and peas. Season. Drop level tablespoons of
dumpling mixture on top of stew.
5 Bake, uncovered, about 20 minutes or until
dumplings are puffed and browned lightly.

CHIVE DUMPLINGS Sift flour into medium bowl;
rub in butter. Stir in cheese and chives, then
enough milk to make a soft sticky dough.

prep + cook time 45 minutes serves 6
nutritional count per serving 19.6g total fat
(9.6g saturated fat); 1910kJ (457 cal);
39.8g carbohydrate; 22g protein; 9.9g fibre

cheese and vegetable polenta bake

45g (1½ ounces) butter
1 medium brown onion (150g), chopped finely
1 clove garlic, crushed
1 medium eggplant (300g), chopped finely
1 medium red capsicum (bell pepper) (200g),
  chopped finely
1 medium green capsicum (bell pepper) (200g),
  chopped finely
100g (3 ounces) button mushrooms,
  chopped finely
410g (13 ounces) canned crushed tomatoes
2 tablespoons finely chopped fresh basil
1 litre (4 cups) water
1⅓ cups (225g) polenta
½ cup (40g) finely grated parmesan cheese
½ cup (60g) coarsely grated cheddar cheese

1 Preheat oven to 220°C/425°F. Oil deep
1.75-litre (7-cup) ovenproof dish.
2 Melt butter in large frying pan; cook onion and
garlic, stirring, until onion softens. Add eggplant,
capsicum, mushrooms and undrained tomatoes;
bring to the boil. Reduce heat; simmer, uncovered,
about 15 minutes or until vegetables are tender
and sauce thickens slightly. Remove from heat; stir
in basil. Season to taste.
3 Meanwhile, bring the water to the boil
in medium saucepan; gradually stir in polenta.
Cook, stirring, about 5 minutes or until polenta
thickens. Stir in cheeses; season to taste.
4 Spread half the polenta mixture over base of
dish; top with vegetable mixture. Spread remaining
polenta mixture over vegetables. Bake about
20 minutes or until browned lightly. Stand
5 minutes before serving.

prep + cook time 55 minutes serves 4
nutritional count per serving 19.3g total fat
(11.5g saturated fat); 1877kJ (449 cal);
49g carbohydrate; 16.6g protein; 6.5g fibre

pumpkin, pea and fetta risotto

500g (1 pound) pumpkin, chopped coarsely
1 tablespoon olive oil
2 cups (500ml) chicken stock
2 cups (500ml) water
1 medium brown onion (150g), chopped finely
2 cloves garlic, crushed
1½ cups (300g) arborio rice
250g (8 ounces) grape tomatoes
1 cup (120g) frozen peas
⅓ cup (25g) finely grated parmesan cheese
100g (3 ounces) soft fetta cheese, crumbled
1 tablespoon coarsely chopped fresh marjoram

1 Preheat oven to 220°C/425°F.
2 Combine pumpkin and half the oil in medium shallow flameproof casserole dish. Roast, uncovered, about 20 minutes or until tender; remove from dish.
3 Reduce oven to 180°C/350°F.
4 Bring stock and the water to the boil in medium saucepan. Reduce heat; simmer, covered.
5 Meanwhile, heat remaining oil in same dish; cook onion and garlic, stirring, until onion softens. Add rice; stir to coat in onion mixture. Stir in simmering stock mixture; cover dish with foil.
6 Bake 25 minutes, stirring halfway through cooking time. Remove risotto from oven; stir in tomatoes and peas. Bake, uncovered, about 10 minutes or until rice is tender. Stir in pumpkin and parmesan; season to taste. Sprinkle with fetta and marjoram.

prep + cook time 1 hour serves 4
nutritional count per serving 13.9g total fat (6.4g saturated fat); 2123kJ (508 cal); 73.7g carbohydrate; 18.4g protein; 6.1g fibre

root vegetable gratin

2 medium potatoes (400g)
2 medium carrots (240g)
2 medium parsnips (500g)
1 small brown onion (80g)
⅔ cup (160ml) pouring cream
⅔ cup (160ml) milk
2 tablespoons finely chopped fresh
  flat-leaf parsley
1 tablespoon horseradish cream
⅓ cup (25g) stale breadcrumbs

1 Preheat oven to 200°C/400°F. Oil deep 1.5 litre (6-cup) ovenproof dish.
2 Using mandolin or V-slicer, cut potato, carrot, parsnip and onion into paper-thin slices. Place potato over base of dish; top with half the onion. Top with carrot, then remaining onion and parsnip.
3 Combine cream, milk, parsley and horseradish cream in large jug; season. Pour cream mixture over vegetables; sprinkle with breadcrumbs.
4 Cover dish with foil; bake about 1¼ hours or until vegetables are tender. Uncover; bake about 30 minutes or until browned lightly. Stand 5 minutes before serving.

prep + cook time 2 hours **serves** 4
nutritional count per serving 20g total fat (12.8g saturated fat); 1496kJ (358 cal); 33.8g carbohydrate; 7.8g protein; 6.3g fibre

kumara, silver beet and mushroom bake

30g (1 ounce) butter
4 trimmed medium silver beet (swiss chard)
  leaves, (140g), shredded coarsely
200g (6½ ounces) button mushrooms, sliced thinly
1 medium brown onion (150g), chopped coarsely
100g (3 ounces) pancetta, chopped coarsely
1 medium kumara (orange sweet potato) (400g)
1 tablespoon plain (all-purpose) flour
½ cup (125ml) pouring cream
½ cup (125ml) milk

1 Preheat oven to 180°C/350°F. Oil deep 20cm (8-inch) square ovenproof dish.
2 Melt half the butter in large frying pan; cook silver beet, stirring, until wilted. Remove from pan.
3 Melt remaining butter in same pan; cook mushrooms, stirring, until browned lightly. Remove from pan.
4 Cook onion and pancetta in same pan, stirring, until onion softens and pancetta is crisp. Remove from pan.
5 Using mandolin or V-slicer, cut kumara into paper-thin slices. Place half the kumara over base of dish. Squeeze excess liquid from silver beet; sprinkle over kumara. Drain liquid from mushrooms; sprinkle over silver beet. Top with pancetta mixture, then remaining kumara.
6 Blend flour with a little of the cream in medium jug; stir in remaining cream and milk. Season. Pour cream mixture over kumara; press down firmly. Cover dish with foil; bake 1 hour. Uncover; bake about 20 minutes or until browned lightly. Stand 5 minutes before serving.

prep + cook time 1 hour 45 minutes **serves** 4
nutritional count per serving 24.7g total fat (15.1g saturated fat); 1450kJ (347 cal); 19g carbohydrate; 11.2g protein; 4g fibre

cauliflower and broccoli gratin

½ small cauliflower (500g), cut into large florets
400g (12½ ounces) broccoli, cut into large florets
60g (2 ounces) butter
¼ cup (35g) plain (all-purpose) flour
3 cups (750ml) hot milk
1 cup (120g) coarsely grated cheddar cheese
½ cup (35g) stale breadcrumbs
½ cup (40g) finely grated parmesan cheese

1 Preheat oven to 220°C/425°F. Oil shallow
1.75-litre (7-cup) ovenproof dish.
2 Boil, steam or microwave cauliflower and
broccoli, separately, until tender; drain.
3 Meanwhile, melt butter in large saucepan.
Add flour; cook, stirring, about 2 minutes or until
mixture bubbles and thickens. Gradually stir in
milk; cook, stirring, until sauce boils and thickens.
Stir in cheddar; season to taste.
4 Place cauliflower and broccoli in dish, pour
cheese sauce over; sprinkle with combined
breadcrumbs and parmesan. Bake, uncovered,
about 20 minutes or until browned lightly.

prep + cook time 45 minutes **serves** 6 (as a side dish)
nutritional count per serving 22.7g total fat
(14.3g saturated fat); 1484kJ (355 cal);
16.4g carbohydrate; 19.1g protein; 5.4g fibre

tip To prevent excess water leaching into the
gratin, steaming is the best method to use for
cooking the vegetables. You can use broccolini
instead of broccoli, if you prefer.
note We've used two ovenproof pans here – each
pan will serve three.

fennel and leek gratin

4 baby fennel bulbs (520g)
1 medium leek (350g), sliced thinly
1½ cups (375ml) pouring cream
½ cup (125ml) milk
45g (1½ ounces) butter
2 tablespoons plain (all-purpose) flour
⅓ cup (40g) coarsely grated cheddar cheese
⅓ cup (25g) finely grated parmesan cheese
⅔ cup (50g) stale breadcrumbs

1 Trim and quarter fennel; reserve 1 tablespoon
finely chopped fennel fronds.
2 Combine fennel, leek, cream and milk in large
saucepan; simmer, covered, about 15 minutes
or until fennel is tender. Transfer fennel and leek
to six shallow 1-cup (250ml) ovenproof dishes;
reserve cream mixture.
3 Preheat oven to 220°C/425°F.
4 Melt butter in same pan. Add flour; cook,
stirring, about 2 minutes or until mixture bubbles
and thickens. Gradually stir in hot cream mixture.
Cook, stirring, until sauce boils and thickens;
season to taste.
5 Pour sauce over fennel; sprinkle with combined
cheeses, breadcrumbs and reserved fennel fronds.
Bake, uncovered, about 15 minutes or until
browned lightly.

prep + cook time 45 minutes **serves** 6 (as a side dish)
nutritional count per serving 38.2g total fat
(24.8g saturated fat); 1839kJ (440 cal);
15.2g carbohydrate; 8.5g protein; 3.7g fibre

serving suggestion Serve with roast lamb, beef or
veal, or your favourite steak.

potatoes

potato gratin with caramelised onion

1 tablespoon olive oil

2 large brown onions (400g), sliced thinly

1 tablespoon light brown sugar

3 teaspoons balsamic vinegar

2 tablespoons coarsely chopped fresh
   flat-leaf parsley

1kg (2 pounds) potatoes

1 tablespoon plain (all-purpose) flour

1¾ cups (430ml) pouring cream

¼ cup (60ml) milk

20g (¾ ounce) butter, chopped finely

¾ cup (90g) coarsely grated gruyère cheese

¾ cup (50g) stale breadcrumbs

1 Heat oil in medium frying pan over low heat; cook onion, stirring occasionally, about 20 minutes or until onion softens. Add sugar and vinegar; cook, stirring occasionally, about 10 minutes or until onion is caramelised. Remove from heat; stir in parsley.

2 Preheat oven to 180°C/350°F. Oil 1.5-litre (6-cup) ovenproof dish.

3 Using mandolin or V-slicer, cut potatoes into paper thin slices; pat dry with absorbent paper. Layer half the potato in dish; top with caramelised onion, then remaining potato.

4 Blend flour with a little of the cream in medium jug; stir in remaining cream and milk. Pour cream mixture over potato mixture; dot with butter. Cover with foil; bake 1¼ hours. Uncover; sprinkle with combined cheese and breadcrumbs. Bake, uncovered, about 15 minutes or until potato is tender. Stand 5 minutes before serving.

prep + cook time 1 hour 45 minutes **serves** 6
nutritional count per serving 42.1g total fat (25.8g saturated fat); 2337kJ (559 cal); 32.9g carbohydrate; 11.5g protein; 3.5g fibre

tip We used sebago potatoes in this recipe.

potatoes with lemon and tomato

1.2kg (2½ pounds) medium potatoes, cut into
  thick wedges
2 medium lemons (280g), sliced thickly
1 tablespoon fresh thyme leaves
½ cup (125ml) dry white wine
2 tablespoons olive oil
480g (15½ ounces) cherry truss tomatoes,
  cut into 5cm (2-inch) lengths
½ cup (80g) seeded kalamata olives
2 tablespoons coarsely chopped fresh
  flat-leaf parsley

1 Preheat oven to 200°C/400°F. Oil 2.5-litre
(10-cup) ovenproof dish.
2 Combine potato, lemon and thyme in dish;
pour over combined wine and oil. Season. Cover
dish with foil; bake 40 minutes. Uncover; bake
30 minutes. Remove from oven; top with tomatoes.
Bake, uncovered, further 12 minutes or until
potato is tender.
3 Serve sprinkled with olives and parsley.

prep + cook time 1 hour 35 minutes serves 6
nutritional count per serving 6.6g total fat
(0.9g saturated fat); 903kJ (216 cal);
26.8g carbohydrate; 4.7g protein; 5.2g fibre

serving suggestion Serve with grilled or
barbecued chicken or fish.

potato, bacon and blue cheese bake

1.2kg (2½ pounds) medium potatoes,
  sliced thickly
2 medium red onions (340g), cut into
  thick wedges
315g (10 ounces) rindless bacon slices,
  chopped coarsely
12 sprigs fresh thyme
¾ cup (180ml) pouring cream
¾ cup (180ml) salt-reduced chicken stock
125g (4 ounces) blue cheese, crumbled

1 Preheat oven to 200°C/400°F. Oil 2.5-litre
(10-cup) ovenproof dish.
2 Combine potato, onion and bacon in dish; top
with half the thyme. Combine cream and stock
in medium jug; season, pour over potato.
3 Bake, uncovered, about 1½ hours or until
potato is tender. Serve topped with cheese
and remaining thyme.

prep + cook time 1 hour 45 minutes serves 6
nutritional count per serving 22.9g total fat
(13.5g saturated fat); 1659kJ (397 cal);
25.6g carbohydrate; 20.5g protein; 3.3g fibre

potato gnocchi with three-cheese sauce

500g (1 pound) potatoes, unpeeled
1 egg, beaten lightly
15g (½ ounce) butter, melted
2 tablespoons finely grated parmesan cheese
1 cup (150g) plain (all-purpose)
  flour, approximately
¼ cup (25g) stale coarse breadcrumbs

THREE-CHEESE SAUCE
1 cup (250ml) pouring cream
½ cup (50g) coarsely grated mozzarella cheese
45g (1½ ounces) gorgonzola cheese, crumbled
½ cup (40g) finely grated parmesan cheese
1 teaspoon dijon mustard
¼ teaspoon ground nutmeg
1 egg yolk
1 tablespoon finely chopped fresh curly parsley

1 Boil or steam whole potatoes until tender; drain. When cool enough to handle, peel away skins. Mash potatoes, using ricer, food mill (mouli) or strainer, into medium bowl; stir in egg, butter, cheese and enough flour to make a firm dough.
2 Divide dough into four portions; roll each portion on floured surface into 2cm (¾in) thick sausage shape. Cut each sausage into 2cm (¾in) pieces; roll pieces into balls.
3 Roll each ball along the tines of a fork, pressing lightly on top of ball with index finger to form classic gnocchi shape – grooved on one side and dimpled on the other. Place gnocchi, in single layer, on lightly floured tray; cover, refrigerate 1 hour.
4 Meanwhile, make three-cheese sauce.
5 Preheat oven to 220°C/425°F. Oil four 1-cup (250ml) ovenproof dishes.
6 Cook gnocchi, in batches, in large saucepan of boiling water until gnocchi float to the surface and are cooked through. Remove from pan with slotted spoon; divide among dishes. Pour sauce over gnocchi; sprinkle with breadcrumbs. Bake, uncovered, about 15 minutes.

THREE-CHEESE SAUCE Combine cream and cheeses in small saucepan; stir over medium heat until smooth. Remove from heat; stir in mustard, nutmeg, egg yolk and parsley. Season to taste.

prep + cook time 1 hour (+ refrigeration)
serves 4
nutritional count per serving 44.3g total fat (27.8g saturated fat); 2537kJ (607 cal); 33.2g carbohydrate; 19.3g protein; 1.8g fibre

serving suggestion Serve with a green salad.
tip We used russet burbank potatoes in this recipe.

mashed potato and bacon bake

2kg (4 pounds) potatoes, chopped coarsely
410g (13 ounces) rindless bacon slices,
 chopped finely
1 cup (240g) sour cream
90g (3 ounces) butter, chopped coarsely
¾ cup (180ml) hot milk
4 green onions (scallions), sliced thinly
2 cups (240g) coarsely grated cheddar cheese

1 Preheat oven to 180°C/350°F. Oil 2.5-litre (10-cup) ovenproof dish.
2 Boil steam or microwave potato until tender; drain.
3 Meanwhile, cook bacon in large frying pan, stirring, until crisp; drain on absorbent paper.
4 Mash potato in large bowl with sour cream, butter and milk until smooth. Stir in half the bacon, half the onion and half the cheese. Season to taste. Spread mixture into dish; sprinkle with remaining bacon, onion and cheese. Bake, uncovered, about 40 minutes or until browned lightly.

prep + cook time 1 hour 20 minutes **serves** 8
nutritional count per serving 36.9g total fat (22.6g saturated fat); 2303kJ (551 cal); 28.9g carbohydrate; 24.5g protein; 3.3g fibre

potato frittata

2 tablespoons olive oil
625g (1¼ pounds) potatoes, chopped coarsely
45g (1½ ounces) baby spinach leaves
2 tablespoons coarsely chopped fresh
   flat-leaf parsley
125g (4 ounces) goat's fetta cheese, crumbled
⅓ cup (25g) coarsely grated parmesan cheese
6 eggs
½ cup (125ml) pouring cream

1 Preheat oven to 200°C/400°F. Oil deep 20cm (8-inch) square cake pan; line base and sides with baking paper; extending paper 5cm (2 inches) over sides. Or, oil deep ovenproof frying pan with base measuring 20cm (8 inches).
2 Heat oil in large frying pan; cook potato, stirring, until browned lightly and almost tender. Drain on absorbent paper.
3 Layer half the spinach, parsley, potato and cheeses in pan; repeat layers. Combine eggs and cream in medium jug; season. Pour egg mixture into pan. Bake about 30 minutes or until set. Stand 5 minutes before serving.

prep + cook time 50 minutes serves 4
nutritional count per serving 39.8g total fat (18.6g saturated fat); 2169kJ (519 cal); 17.8g carbohydrate; 21.7g protein; 2.4g fibre

tip We used desiree potatoes in this recipe.

creamy potato and bacon bake

1.2kg (2½ pounds) potatoes
200g (6½ ounces) rindless bacon slices,
  chopped finely
¼ cup finely chopped fresh chives
1 cup (250ml) pouring cream
¾ cup (180ml) chicken stock
¾ cup (90g) coarsely grated cheddar cheese

1 Preheat oven to 180°C/350°F. Oil 1.5-litre
(6-cup) ovenproof dish.
2 Using mandolin or V-slicer, cut potatoes
into paper-thin slices; pat dry with absorbent
paper. Layer a quarter of the potato in dish; top
with one-third of the bacon and chives. Continue
layering remaining potato, bacon and chives,
finishing with potato.
3 Heat cream and stock in small saucepan
until almost boiling; pour over potatoes. Cover
with foil; bake 40 minutes. Uncover; bake
20 minutes. Sprinkle with cheese; bake about
20 minutes or until potato is tender. Stand
10 minutes before serving.

prep + cook time 1 hour 50 minutes **serves** 6
nutritional count per serving 26.3g total fat
(16.3g saturated fat); 1651kJ (395 cal);
22.7g carbohydrate; 15.6g protein; 2.6g fibre

tip We used desiree potatoes in this recipe.

moroccan sweet potato bake

1 medium lemon (140g)
¾ cup firmly packed fresh coriander leaves
¼ cup (60ml) olive oil
6 cloves garlic, quartered
2 teaspoons sweet paprika
½ teaspoon ground cumin
¼ teaspoon cayenne pepper
1 cup (250ml) chicken stock
1.5kg (3 pounds) kumara (orange sweet potato),
  cut into thick wedges
1 cup (70g) stale breadcrumbs
2 tablespoons finely chopped fresh
  flat-leaf parsley

1 Preheat oven to 200°C/400°F. Oil 2-litre (8-cup)
ovenproof dish.
2 Finely grate rind from lemon, you need
2 teaspoons. Squeeze juice from lemon, you
need 2 tablespoons. Blend or process coriander,
2 tablespoons of the oil, juice, garlic and spices
until smooth.
3 Combine spice paste, stock and kumara in large
bowl; season. Transfer mixture to dish. Cover with
foil; bake 1 hour 10 minutes. Remove foil; sprinkle
with combined breadcrumbs, parsley, lemon
rind and remaining oil. Bake, uncovered, about
20 minutes or until sweet potato is tender. Stand
5 minutes before serving.

prep + cook time 1 hour 50 minutes **serves** 8
nutritional count per serving 7.5g total fat
(1.1g saturated fat); 857kJ (205 cal);
27.8g carbohydrate; 4.7g protein; 3.6g fibre

twice-baked potatoes

8 medium potatoes (1.6kg), unpeeled
200g (6½ ounces) rindless bacon slices,
  chopped finely
125g (4 ounces) canned creamed corn
¼ cup (60g) sour cream
2 green onions (scallions), sliced thinly
1 cup (120g) coarsely grated cheddar cheese

1 Preheat oven to 180°C/350°F.
2 Pierce skin of each potato with a skewer or fork;
wrap each potato in foil, place in baking-paper-
lined large shallow baking dish. Bake, uncovered,
about 1 hour and 20 minutes or until tender.
3 Meanwhile, cook bacon in medium frying pan
until crisp. Drain on absorbent paper.

4 Cut a shallow slice from each potato; scoop
flesh from each top into medium bowl, discard skin.
Scoop about two-thirds of the flesh from each
potato into same bowl; place potato shells
in same baking dish.
5 Mash potato until smooth; stir in creamed corn,
sour cream, bacon, half the onion and half the
cheese. Divide mixture into potato shells; sprinkle
with remaining onion and cheese. Bake, uncovered,
about 20 minutes or until heated through.

prep + cook time 1 hour 55 minutes serves 4
nutritional count per serving 21g total fat
(12g saturated fat); 2115kJ (506 cal);
48.3g carbohydrate; 26.6g protein; 6.3g fibre

ham, potato, leek and artichoke bake

45g (1½ ounces) butter
2 tablespoons plain (all-purpose) flour
2 cups (500ml) hot chicken stock
1kg (2 pounds) potatoes, sliced thickly
2 medium leeks (700g), sliced thickly
200g (6½ ounces) leg ham, chopped coarsely
280g (9 ounces) bottled artichoke hearts in
   brine, drained, halved
1 cup (80g) coarsely grated parmesan cheese

1 Preheat oven to 200°C/400°F. Oil 2-litre (8-cup)
ovenproof dish.
2 Melt butter in medium saucepan. Add flour;
cook, stirring, about 2 minutes or until mixture
bubbles and thickens. Gradually stir in stock; cook
sauce, stirring, until mixture boils and thickens.
Season to taste.

3 Layer half the potato in dish; top with leek,
ham, artichokes and the remaining potato. Pour
sauce over potato. Cover dish with foil; bake
1 hour 20 minutes. Uncover; sprinkle with cheese.
Bake about 30 minutes or until potato is tender.
Stand 10 minutes before serving.

prep + cook time 2 hours serves 8
nutritional count per serving 9.6g total fat
(5.6g saturated fat); 970kJ (232 cal);
19.6g carbohydrate; 14.2g protein; 5.1g fibre

fish

tuna and asparagus crumble

45g (1½ ounces) butter
2 medium leeks (700g), chopped finely
340g (11 ounces) asparagus, chopped coarsely
1 cup (250ml) pouring cream
425g (13½ ounces) canned tuna in springwater,
  drained, flaked

CRUMBLE OAT TOPPING
⅔ cup (60g) rolled oats
⅓ cup (40g) coarsely grated cheddar cheese
2 tablespoons plain (all-purpose) flour
30g (1 ounce) butter, chopped finely

1 Make crumble oat topping.
2 Preheat oven to 240°C/475°F.
3 Melt butter in large frying pan; cook leek, stirring, 2 minutes. Add asparagus; cook, covered, about 5 minutes or until asparagus is tender. Add cream and tuna; bring to the boil. Season to taste.
4 Spoon mixture into four 1¼-cup (310ml) ovenproof dishes; sprinkle with topping. Bake about 20 minutes or until browned lightly.

CRUMBLE OAT TOPPING Process ingredients until coarsely chopped.

prep + cook time 45 minutes serves 4
nutritional count per serving 52g total fat (32.5g saturated fat); 2909kJ (696 cal); 23g carbohydrate; 31.5g protein; 8.3g fibre

note We used larger dishes here – each dish will serve two.

salmon and zucchini lasagne

45g (1½ ounces) butter
¼ cup (35g) plain (all-purpose) flour
2 cups (500ml) hot milk
1 cup (240g) ricotta cheese
3 green onions (scallions), chopped finely
2 tablespoons finely chopped fresh mint
2 large zucchini (300g), sliced thinly lengthways
3 fresh lasagne sheets (150g)
400g (12½ ounces) skinless salmon fillet,
 sliced thinly
½ cup (50g) coarsely grated mozzarella cheese

1 Preheat oven to 220°C/425°F.
2 Melt butter in medium saucepan. Add flour; cook, stirring, about 2 minutes or until mixture bubbles and thickens. Gradually stir in milk; cook, stirring, until sauce boils and thickens. Season to taste. Spoon 1 cup white sauce into medium bowl; stir in ricotta, onion and mint.
3 Cook zucchini in large saucepan of boiling, salted water for 2 minutes. Drain zucchini in a single layer on absorbent paper. Cook pasta, in batches, in same pan of boiling water for about 30 seconds or until tender; drain.
4 Spread ⅓ cup white sauce over base of 1-litre (4-cup) ovenproof dish. Top with a lasagne sheet, half the zucchini, then half the fish and half the ricotta mixture. Repeat layering, seasoning lightly between layers, with remaining lasagne, zucchini, fish and ricotta mixture, finishing with a lasagne sheet. Top with remaining white sauce; sprinkle with mozzarella. Bake, uncovered, about 20 minutes or until browned lightly.

prep + cook time 50 minutes **serves** 4
nutritional count per serving 31.5g total fat (17.1g saturated fat); 2541kJ (608 cal); 40.4g carbohydrate; 39.6g protein; 3.1g fibre

tips To ensure the fish doesn't overcook during the baking time, you need to pre-cook the zucchini and pasta. As cooked, drained lasagne sheets tend to stick together, it's better to cook each sheet just before using it.

spicy sardine and spaghetti bake

250g (8 ounces) spaghetti
1 cup (70g) stale breadcrumbs
⅓ cup finely chopped fresh flat-leaf parsley
⅓ cup (80ml) olive oil
318g (10 ounces) canned sardines in oil, drained
250g (8 ounces) cherry tomatoes,
  chopped coarsely
4 cloves garlic, crushed
1½ teaspoons dried chilli flakes

1   Preheat oven to 220°C/425°F.
2   Cook pasta in large saucepan of boiling
water until tender; drain, reserve ⅓ cup (80ml)
cooking liquid.
3   Combine breadcrumbs, parsley and
1 tablespoon of the oil in medium bowl.
4   Heat remaining oil in same pan; cook sardines,
tomato, garlic and chilli, stirring, until tomato
begins to soften. Stir in pasta; season to taste.
5   Spoon mixture into 2-litre (8-cup) ovenproof
dish; pour over reserved cooking liquid. Sprinkle
with breadcrumb mixture. Bake, uncovered, about
10 minutes or until browned lightly.

prep + cook time 30 minutes serves 4
nutritional count per serving 29.7g total fat
(6.1g saturated fat); 2500kJ (598 cal);
56.3g carbohydrate; 24g protein; 4.6g fibre

tip Seasoning a dish with pepper when it already
contains chilli isn't doubling up, as they both have
distinct flavours.

baked seafood risotto

1 litre (4 cups) fish stock
1 tablespoon olive oil
1 medium brown onion (150g), chopped finely
2 cloves garlic, crushed
1½ cups (300g) arborio rice
½ cup (125ml) dry white wine
700g (1½ pounds) marinara mix
250g (8 ounces) rocket (arugula), trimmed,
  chopped coarsely
30g (1 ounce) butter, chopped finely

1 Preheat oven to 200°C/400°F.
2 Bring stock to the boil in medium saucepan.
3 Meanwhile, heat oil in 2-litre (8-cup) paella pan or ovenproof deep frying pan; cook onion, stirring, until soft. Add garlic; cook, stirring, until fragrant. Add rice; stir to coat in onion mixture. Add wine; simmer, uncovered, until liquid is absorbed. Add 3 cups (750ml) of hot stock; season.
4 Bake, uncovered, 15 minutes. Stir in marinara mix and remaining hot stock. Bake, uncovered, about 25 minutes, stirring halfway through cooking time, or until rice is tender. Stir in rocket and butter.

prep + cook time 1 hour **serves** 4
nutritional count per serving 17.3g total fat
(6.6g saturated fat); 2638kJ (631 cal);
65.4g carbohydrate; 46.9g protein; 2.5g fibre

fish provençale

1 tablespoon olive oil
1 medium brown onion (150g), chopped finely
3 cloves garlic, crushed
1 cup (250g) bottled tomato pasta sauce
2 tablespoons finely chopped fresh basil
⅓ cup (80ml) fish stock
500g (1 pound) potatoes
2 small eggplant (460g), sliced thinly
2 large zucchini (300g), sliced thinly
350g (11 ounces) skinless white fish fillets, sliced thickly

1 Preheat oven to 220°C/425°F.
2 Heat oil in medium saucepan; cook onion, stirring, until soft. Add garlic; cook, stirring, until fragrant. Add sauce and basil; simmer, uncovered, 5 minutes. Stir in stock; season to taste.
3 Meanwhile, boil, steam or microwave potatoes until tender; drain. When cool enough to handle, slice thinly.
4 Heat oiled grill plate (or grill or barbecue); cook eggplant until browned lightly.
5 Spoon half the tomato mixture into 2-litre (8-cup) ovenproof dish; layer potato, zucchini, eggplant and fish in rows in dish. Pour remaining tomato mixture into dish. Bake, uncovered, about 15 minutes or until fish is cooked.

prep + cook time 1 hour **serves** 4
nutritional count per serving 8.3g total fat (1.4g saturated fat); 1204kJ (288 cal); 24.8g carbohydrate; 24.4g protein; 7.8g fibre

note We used two smaller dishes here – each dish serves two.

smoked haddock potato bake

500g (1 pound) potatoes
70g (2½ ounces) butter
1 medium brown onion (150g), chopped finely
2 stalks celery (300g), trimmed, sliced thinly
2 tablespoons plain (all-purpose) flour
1 cup (250ml) fish stock
500g (1 pound) smoked haddock, skinned,
  chopped coarsely
1 cup (120g) frozen peas
½ cup (125ml) pouring cream
2 tablespoons coarsely chopped fresh
  flat-leaf parsley

1 Preheat oven to 220°C/425°F.
2 Boil, steam or microwave potatoes until almost tender; drain. When cool enough to handle, slice thinly.
3 Meanwhile, melt 50g (1½ ounces) of the butter in large saucepan; cook onion and celery, stirring, until onion softens. Add flour; cook, stirring, about 2 minutes or until mixture bubbles and thickens. Gradually stir in stock; cook, stirring, until mixture boils and thickens. Remove from heat; stir in fish, peas, cream and parsley. Season to taste.
4 Spoon mixture into shallow 1.5-litre (6-cup) ovenproof dish; top with potato. Brush with remaining melted butter. Bake, uncovered, about 25 minutes or until browned lightly.

prep + cook time 50 minutes **serves** 6
nutritional count per serving 19.7g total fat (12.5g saturated fat); 1430kJ (342 cal); 15.6g carbohydrate; 24.1g protein; 3.6g fibre

tip We used desiree potatoes in this recipe. Season this dish carefully as the haddock and stock are already salty.

salmon bread and butter pudding

8 large slices white bread (500g), crusts removed
45g (1½ ounces) butter, softened
150g (4½ ounces) piece hot-smoked salmon,
  flaked
4 eggs
2 cups (500ml) milk
1 cup (250ml) pouring cream
2 tablespoons finely chopped fresh chives
2 teaspoons finely chopped fresh tarragon
1 tablespoon dijon mustard
½ cup (60g) coarsely grated cheddar cheese

1 Preheat oven to 200°C/400°F. Grease 2-litre (8-cup) ovenproof dish.
2 Spread both sides of bread with butter; cut into triangles. Layer bread, slightly overlapping, in dish; sprinkle with salmon.
3 Whisk eggs, milk, cream, chives, tarragon, mustard and half the cheese in medium bowl until combined; season. Pour half the egg mixture over bread. Stand 1 hour.
4 Pour remaining egg mixture into dish; sprinkle with remaining cheese. Place ovenproof dish in large baking dish. Add enough hot water to baking dish to come halfway up the sides of ovenproof dish. Cover loosely with foil; bake 25 minutes. Uncover; bake about 20 minutes or until set. Remove pudding from baking dish. Stand 5 minutes before serving.

prep + cook time 1 hour (+ standing) serves 4
nutritional count per serving 56.5g total fat (32.8g saturated fat); 3800kJ (909 cal); 64.3g carbohydrate; 35.3g protein; 3.8g fibre

sardine, potato and lemon bake

¼ cup (60ml) olive oil
1kg (2 pounds) potatoes, peeled, sliced thinly
1 tablespoon honey
1 tablespoon finely chopped preserved
  lemon rind
1 teaspoon harissa paste
10 fresh sardine fillets (375g)

1 Preheat oven to 220°C/425°F.
2 Heat oil in large frying pan; cook potato, in batches, stirring, about 10 minutes or until browned lightly. Drain oil from potato over medium heatproof bowl; stir honey, rind and harissa into bowl, season.
3 Layer potato and sardines in 1.5-litre (6-cup) ovenproof dish. Pour honey mixture into dish. Bake, uncovered, about 20 minutes or until sardines are cooked.

prep + cook time 40 minutes **serves** 4
nutritional count per serving 23.9g total fat (4.6g saturated fat); 1898kJ (454 cal); 32.6g carbohydrate; 25.3g protein; 3.4g fibre

tip A mandolin or V-slicer is ideal to quickly slice potatoes evenly. Rinse the sliced potato in cold water to remove the starch and avoid the slices sticking together during cooking. Drain slices, then pat dry with absorbent paper before cooking.

creamy fish and potato bake

3 cups (750ml) milk
3 cloves garlic, crushed
1kg (2 pounds) potatoes, sliced thinly
45g (1½ ounces) butter, chopped finely
2 medium brown onions (300g), sliced thinly
2 tablespoons plain (all-purpose) flour
500g (1 pound) skinless white fish fillets,
 sliced thickly

1 Preheat oven to 220°C/425°F.
2 Combine milk and garlic in large saucepan;
bring almost to the boil. Season. Add potato;
simmer, stirring occasionally, about 15 minutes or
until potato is tender. Drain over large heatproof
bowl; reserve milk mixture.
3 Melt butter in large frying pan; cook onion,
stirring, until soft. Add flour; cook, stirring, about
2 minutes or until mixture bubbles and thickens.
Gradually stir in reserved milk; cook, stirring, until
mixture boils and thickens. Stir in potato.
4 Divide half the potato mixture into six
1-cup (250ml) shallow ovenproof dishes; top
with fish, then remaining potato mixture.
Bake, uncovered, about 15 minutes or until
fish is cooked.

prep + cook time 50 minutes **serves** 6
nutritional count per serving 13.1g total fat
(7.9g saturated fat); 1442kJ (345 cal);
29.3g carbohydrate; 25.7g protein; 3.2g fibre

tips We used blue-eye fish and desiree potatoes in
this recipe. A mandolin or V-slicer is ideal for thinly
slicing potatoes. As you need the starch from the
potatoes in this recipe, don't rinse them after
slicing. To stop them turning brown, add them to
the hot milk and garlic as soon as they are sliced.
note We used two large dishes here – each will
serve three.

This is a take on the Russian coulibiac salmon pie. It's important to season each element (rice, fish and silver beet). Choose a fillet approximately the same length as the dish or buy a thicker piece and butterfly it. To see if salmon is cooked, insert a knife through centre of pie and check temperature on your wrist; it should feel hot.

salmon, silver beet and rice pie

¼ cup (60ml) olive oil
1 large brown onion (200g), chopped finely
1½ cups (300g) jasmine rice
2¼ cups (560ml) water
2 eggs
1kg (2 pounds) silver beet (swiss chard), trimmed
500g (1 pound) skinless salmon fillet
2 cloves garlic, crushed
⅓ cup (80ml) thickened (heavy) cream
1 sheet puff pastry

1 Heat 2 tablespoons of the oil in medium saucepan; cook onion, stirring, until soft. Add rice; stir to coat in onion mixture. Add the water; bring to the boil. Reduce heat to medium-low; cook, covered, about 13 minutes or until water is absorbed and rice is tender. Transfer rice mixture to baking-paper-lined oven tray to cool.

2 Meanwhile, boil eggs in small saucepan of water for 6 minutes. Drain; rinse under cold water. Shell and halve eggs.

3 Preheat oven to 220°C/425°F. Grease shallow 1.25-litre (5-cup) square ovenproof dish.

4 Heat large frying pan; cook silver beet, stirring, until wilted. Remove from pan. When cool enough to handle, squeeze excess liquid from silver beet; chop coarsely.

5 Season salmon. Heat remaining oil in same pan; cook salmon on both sides until browned. Remove from pan. Add silver beet and garlic to same pan; cook, stirring, until fragrant. Stir in cream; season to taste.

6 Spread half the rice in dish; cover with half the silver beet. Top with salmon; place eggs along centre of salmon, cover with remaining silver beet to form a slight dome; cover with remaining rice. Cut pastry to fit dish; cover with pastry, tucking edges inside dish. Bake, uncovered, about 30 minutes or until browned lightly.

prep + cook time 1 hour 10 minutes **serves** 6
nutritional count per serving 28.7g total fat
(6.9g saturated fat); 2462kJ (589 cal);
53.7g carbohydrate; 26.8g protein; 4.5g fibre

spicy tuna pasta bake

300g (9½ ounces) cannelloni tubes
2 tablespoons olive oil
3 cloves garlic, crushed
4 drained anchovy fillets, chopped finely
2 cups (500g) bottled tomato pasta sauce
½ cup (75g) seeded kalamata olives, halved
2 tablespoons finely chopped fresh oregano
1 tablespoon rinsed, drained capers
½ teaspoon dried chilli flakes
425g (13½ ounces) canned tuna in oil,
  drained, flaked
¼ cup (25g) coarsely grated mozzarella cheese
¼ cup (20g) finely grated parmesan cheese

1 Preheat oven to 220°C/425°F.
2 Cook pasta in large saucepan of boiling water until tender; drain, reserving ¼ cup (60ml) of cooking liquid.
3 Meanwhile, heat oil in large saucepan; cook garlic and anchovy, stirring, until fragrant. Stir in sauce, olives, oregano, capers and chilli; simmer, uncovered, 5 minutes. Season to taste. Stir in pasta, tuna and the reserved cooking liquid.
4 Spoon mixture into 2-litre (8-cup) ovenproof dish; sprinkle with combined cheeses. Bake, uncovered, about 15 minutes or until browned lightly.

prep + cook time 35 minutes serves 4
nutritional count per serving 26.5g total fat (5.3g saturated fat); 2730kJ (653 cal); 66g carbohydrate; 34.6g protein; 6g fibre

tuna and corn bake

200g (6½ ounces) rigatoni pasta
45g (1½ ounces) butter
1½ tablespoons plain (all-purpose) flour
2½ cups (625ml) hot milk
1½ cups (180g) coarsely grated cheddar cheese
420g (13½ ounces) canned corn kernels, drained
425g (13½ ounces) canned tuna in springwater,
  drained, flaked
1 cup (120g) frozen peas
2 green onions (scallions), chopped finely
2 tablespoons finely chopped fresh
  flat-leaf parsley
2 tablespoons lemon juice

1 Preheat oven to 220°C/425°F.
2 Cook pasta in large saucepan of boiling water until tender; drain.
3 Meanwhile, melt butter in medium saucepan. Add flour; cook, stirring, about 2 minutes or until mixture bubbles and thickens. Gradually stir in milk; cook, stirring, until sauce boils and thickens. Stir in pasta, ⅓ cup (40g) of the cheese, corn, tuna, peas, onion, parsley and juice; season to taste.
4 Spoon mixture into 2-litre (8-cup) ovenproof dish; sprinkle with remaining cheese. Bake, uncovered, about 25 minutes or until browned lightly.

prep + cook time 40 minutes serves 6
nutritional count per serving 22.8g total fat
(13.9g saturated fat); 2103kJ (503 cal);
41.2g carbohydrate; 31.2g protein; 4.5g fibre

chicken

chicken, sausage and bean cassoulet

1kg (2 pounds) chicken pieces
½ cup (75g) plain (all-purpose) flour
¼ cup (60ml) olive oil
10 pork chipolata sausages (300g)
1 medium brown onion (150g), chopped coarsely
1 large carrot (180g), chopped coarsely
2 cloves garlic, sliced thinly
4 sprigs fresh thyme
1 bay leaf
2 tablespoons tomato paste
800g (1½ pounds) canned diced tomatoes
1 cup (250ml) chicken stock
840g (1¾ pounds) canned white beans, rinsed, drained
1 cup (70g) stale breadcrumbs
2 tablespoons finely chopped fresh flat-leaf parsley

1 Preheat oven to 200°C/400°F.
2 Coat chicken in flour; shake off excess. Heat half the oil in large flameproof casserole dish; cook chicken, in batches, until browned. Remove from dish.
3 Cook sausages, in same dish until browned. Remove from dish.
4 Heat remaining oil in same dish; cook onion, carrot, garlic, thyme and bay leaf, stirring, until onion softens. Add paste; cook, stirring, 1 minute. Return chicken and sausages to dish with undrained tomatoes and stock; bring to the boil. Cover; bake 20 minutes. Remove from oven; stir in beans. Cover; bake 30 minutes or until sauce thickens and chicken is tender. Season to taste. Preheat grill (broiler).
5 Sprinkle cassoulet with combined breadcrumbs and parsley; place under grill until browned lightly.

prep + cook time 1 hour 25 minutes **serves** 8
nutritional count per serving 26.2g total fat (7.7g saturated fat); 1756kJ (420cal); 21.6g carbohydrate; 22.6g protein; 5g fibre

chicken and sweet corn bake

3 cups (480g) coarsely chopped
 barbecued chicken
420g (13½ ounces) canned creamed corn
1½ cup (180g) coarsely grated cheddar cheese
½ cup (125ml) pouring cream
4 green onions (scallions), sliced thinly
1 cup (70g) stale breadcrumbs

tip You need to purchase a large barbecued
chicken to get the amount of shredded meat
required for this recipe.

1 Preheat oven to 220°C/425°F.
2 Combine chicken, corn, cheese, cream and
onion in large bowl; season. Spoon mixture into
four oiled 1-cup (250ml) ovenproof dishes; sprinkle
with breadcrumbs.
3 Place dishes on oven tray; bake about
20 minutes or until browned lightly.

prep + cook time 25 minutes **serves** 4
nutritional count per serving 26.9g total fat
(14.4g saturated fat); 2006kJ (480cal);
27.2g carbohydrate; 30.4g protein; 5.1g fibre

chicken and eggplant parmigiana

2 chicken breast fillets (400g)
2 tablespoons olive oil
1 medium eggplant (300g), sliced thinly
4 trimmed medium silver beet (swiss chard)
  leaves, (320g)
1⅔ cups (400g) bottled tomato pasta sauce
1 cup (100g) coarsely grated mozzarella cheese
⅓ cup (25g) finely grated parmesan cheese

1 Preheat oven to 220°C/ 425°F.
2 Cut chicken breasts in half horizontally.
Combine chicken and half the oil in large bowl.
Cook chicken on heated oiled grill plate (or grill
or barbecue) until browned both sides. Place in
oiled 1.5-litre (6-cup) ovenproof dish.

3 Cook eggplant on heated oiled grill plate (or
grill or barbecue), brushing with remaining oil,
until browned and tender.
4 Meanwhile, boil, steam or microwave silver beet
about 30 seconds or until just tender; transfer to
bowl of iced water. Drain; squeeze excess water
from silver beet. Drain on absorbent paper.
5 Top chicken with silver beet and eggplant,
then sauce; sprinkle with combined cheeses.
Bake, uncovered, about 20 minutes or until
browned lightly.

prep + cook time 45 minutes serves 4
nutritional count per serving 20.2g total fat
(6.7g saturated fat); 1555kJ (372cal);
10.5g carbohydrate; 34.9g protein; 5.4g fibre

serving suggestion Serve with a green salad.

red curry chicken risotto

1 tablespoon peanut oil
500g (1 pound) chicken thigh fillets,
  chopped coarsely
1 medium brown onion (150g), chopped finely
1 medium red capsicum (bell pepper) (200g),
  chopped coarsely
1 fresh long red chilli, sliced thinly
3 cloves garlic, crushed
1½ cups (300g) arborio rice
¼ cup (75g) red curry paste
2 cups (500ml) chicken stock
½ cup (125ml) water
4 kaffir lime leaves, sliced thinly
1 cup (250ml) coconut cream
125g (4 ounces) green beans, trimmed, halved
30g (1 ounce) baby spinach leaves,
  chopped coarsely
¼ cup loosely packed fresh coriander
  (cilantro) leaves

1 Preheat oven to 200°C/400°F.
2 Heat oil in large flameproof casserole dish;
cook chicken until browned. Remove from dish.
3 Heat remaining oil in same dish; cook onion,
capsicum, chilli and garlic, stirring, until onion
softens. Add rice and paste; cook, stirring,
1 minute.
4 Return chicken to dish with stock, the water and
lime leaves. Cover with foil; bake about 50 minutes,
stirring occasionally, or until rice is tender. Remove
dish from oven; stir in coconut cream, beans and
spinach. Cover; stand 10 minutes. Season to taste;
serve sprinkled with coriander.

prep + cook time 1 hour 15 minutes serves 4
nutritional count per serving 32.6g total fat
(15.4g saturated fat); 2980kJ (713cal);
68.7g carbohydrate; 33.8g protein; 5.5g fibre

tip Use whichever type of curry paste you prefer.

creamy chicken, bacon and corn chowder

45g (1½ ounces) butter
2 rindless bacon slices (130g), chopped finely
1 medium leek (350g), sliced thinly
2 stalks celery (300g), trimmed, chopped finely
1 medium carrot (120g), chopped finely
¼ cup (35g) plain (all-purpose) flour
2 cups (500ml) hot milk
½ cup (125ml) pouring cream
2 medium potatoes (400g), chopped coarsely
1 fresh bay leaf
2 chicken breast fillets (400g), chopped coarsely
310g (10 ounces) canned corn kernels,
  rinsed, drained
2 tablespoons finely chopped fresh chives
200g (6½ ounces) crusty bread, cut into
  small cubes

1 Preheat oven to 200°C/400°F.
2 Melt butter in large saucepan; cook bacon, leek,
celery and carrot, stirring, until vegetables soften.
Add flour; cook, stirring, 1 minute. Gradually stir
in milk and cream; stir in potato and bay leaf. Cook,
stirring, until mixture boils and thickens. Simmer,
uncovered, about 5 minutes or until potato is
tender. Stir in chicken, corn and chives.
3 Spoon mixture into 2-litre (8-cup) ovenproof
dish; sprinkle with bread. Bake, uncovered, about
30 minutes or until browned lightly.

prep + cook time 1 hour **serves** 6
nutritional count per serving 21.8g total fat
(12.5g saturated fat); 2073kJ (496cal);
42.1g carbohydrate; 30g protein; 6.1g fibre

tip Discard bay leaf before serving.

mexican chicken tortilla bake

1 tablespoon olive oil
1 large red onion (300g), sliced thinly
1 medium red capsicum (bell pepper) (200g),
  sliced thinly
800g (1½ pounds) canned diced tomatoes
420g (13½ ounces) canned kidney beans,
  rinsed, drained
310g (10 ounces) canned corn kernels,
  rinsed, drained
35g (1 ounce) taco seasoning
2 cups (320g) shredded barbecued chicken
⅓ cup coarsely chopped fresh coriander (cilantro)
4 x 19cm (7½-inch) flour tortillas
¾ cup (75g) coarsely grated mozzarella cheese

1 Preheat oven to 220°C/425°F.
2 Heat oil in large saucepan; cook onion and
capsicum, stirring, until tender. Add undrained
tomatoes, beans, corn and seasoning; simmer,
uncovered, about 10 minutes or until thickened
slightly. Add chicken and coriander; cook,
stirring, until hot. Season to taste.

3 Line base and sides of 20cm (8-inch) springform
pan with foil or baking paper; place on oven tray.
Line base of pan with a tortilla; top with one-third
of the chicken mixture. Repeat layering with
remaining tortillas and chicken mixture, finishing
with a tortilla; sprinkle with cheese. Bake, uncovered,
about 20 minutes until browned lightly. Stand
5 minutes before cutting.

prep + cook time 45 minutes **serves** 6
nutritional count per serving 13.2g total fat
(3.9g saturated fat); 1572kJ (376cal);
33.8g carbohydrate; 26.4g protein; 8.1g fibre

serving suggestion Serve with an avocado salad
or guacamole.
note You need to buy half large barbecued chicken
(450g) to get the amount of shredded meat required
for this recipe.

cheesy chicken, tomato and bacon rigatoni

315g (10 ounces) rigatoni pasta
2 tablespoons olive oil
500g (1 pound) chicken tenderloins, sliced thinly
1 medium red onion (170g), sliced thinly
4 rindless bacon slices (260g), chopped coarsely
2 cups (500g) bottled tomato pasta sauce
¼ cup finely chopped fresh basil
1½ cups (180g) coarsely grated cheddar cheese

1 Preheat oven to 220°C/425°F.
2 Cook pasta in large saucepan of boiling water until tender; drain. Return to pan.
3 Meanwhile, heat half the oil in large frying pan; cook chicken until browned. Remove from pan.

4 Heat remaining oil in same pan; cook onion and bacon, stirring, until bacon is crisp. Return chicken to pan with sauce; simmer, uncovered, 10 minutes. Stir in basil; season to taste.
5 Stir chicken mixture and half the cheese into pasta. Spoon pasta mixture into 2-litre (8-cup) ovenproof dish; sprinkle with remaining cheese. Bake, uncovered, about 15 minutes or until browned lightly.

prep + cook time 50 minutes **serves** 4
nutritional count per serving 34.9g total fat (14g saturated fat); 3540kJ (847cal); 65.8g carbohydrate; 64g protein; 6g fibre

chicken cacciatore with gremolata and parmesan topping

1.5kg (3 pounds) chicken pieces
⅓ cup (50g) plain (all-purpose) flour
2 tablespoons olive oil
1 large red onion (300g), chopped coarsely
2 cloves garlic, crushed
1 medium red capsicum (bell pepper) (200g), sliced thickly
½ cup (125ml) dry white wine
410g (13 ounces) canned diced tomatoes
410g (13 ounces) canned cherry tomatoes in tomato juice
½ cup (125ml) chicken stock
2 tablespoons tomato paste
1 teaspoon caster (superfine) sugar
½ cup (80g) seeded black olives

GREMOLATA AND PARMESAN TOPPING
½ cup (40g) coarsely grated parmesan cheese
⅓ cup finely chopped fresh flat-leaf parsley
1 tablespoon finely grated lemon rind
1 clove garlic, crushed

1 Preheat oven to 200°C/400°F.
2 Coat chicken in flour; shake off excess. Heat oil in large deep flameproof casserole dish; cook chicken, in batches, until browned. Remove from dish.
3 Cook onion, garlic and capsicum in same dish, stirring, until onion softens. Add wine; simmer, uncovered, until liquid is reduced by half. Stir in undrained tomatoes, stock, paste and sugar.
4 Return chicken to dish; bring to the boil. Cover; bake 45 minutes. Uncover; bake about 45 minutes or until chicken is tender and sauce has thickened. Skim fat from surface; stir in olives. Season to taste.
5 Meanwhile, make gremolata and parmesan topping. Sprinkle over dish just before serving.

GREMOLATA AND PARMESAN TOPPING
Combine ingredients in a small bowl.

prep + cook time 1 hour 50 minutes serves 6
nutritional count per serving 29.1g total fat (8.6g saturated fat); 2019kJ (483cal); 19g carbohydrate; 31.4g protein; 3.8g fibre

serving suggestion Serve with steamed rice or cooked pasta of your choice.

chicken, zucchini and mushroom lasagne

⅓ cup (80ml) olive oil
1 medium brown onion (150g), chopped finely
2 cloves garlic, crushed
500g (1 pound) minced (ground) chicken
2 tablespoons tomato paste
410g (13 ounces) canned diced tomatoes
1 teaspoon caster (superfine) sugar
⅓ cup coarsely chopped fresh basil
3 medium zucchini (360g), sliced thinly
5 flat mushrooms (400g), sliced thinly
375g (12 ounces) fresh lasagne sheets
⅓ cup (25g) finely grated parmesan cheese

WHITE SAUCE
60g (2 ounces) butter
¼ cup (35g) plain (all-purpose) flour
2¼ cups (560ml) hot milk
⅓ cup (25g) finely grated parmesan cheese

1 Preheat oven to 200°C/400°F.
2 Heat 1 tablespoon of the oil in medium saucepan; cook onion and garlic, stirring, until onion softens. Add chicken; stir until browned. Add paste, undrained tomatoes and sugar; bring to the boil. Reduce heat; simmer, uncovered, 5 minutes. Stir in basil; season.
3 Cook zucchini and mushrooms, in batches, on heated oiled grill plate (or grill or barbecue), brushing with remaining oil, until browned and tender.
4 Meanwhile, make white sauce.
5 Line base of 2-litre (8-cup) ovenproof dish with lasagne sheets, trimming to fit. Top with one-third of the chicken mixture, half the vegetable mixture and half the white sauce. Top with lasagne sheets, trimming to fit. Top with half the remaining chicken mixture, remaining vegetable mixture, lasagne sheets, then remaining chicken mixture. Top with remaining lasagne sheets and remaining white sauce; sprinkle with cheese.
6 Cover dish with foil; bake 20 minutes. Uncover; bake about 30 minutes or until browned lightly. Stand 10 minutes before serving.

WHITE SAUCE Melt butter in medium saucepan. Add flour; cook, stirring, 2 minutes. Remove from heat; gradually stir in milk. Cook, stirring, until sauce boils and thickens. Simmer, uncovered, 3 minutes. Season to taste. Remove from heat; stir in cheese.

prep + cook time 1 hour 15 minutes serves 6
nutritional count per serving 34.8g total fat (13.4g saturated fat); 2909kJ (696cal); 59.8g carbohydrate; 34.4g protein; 6.6g fibre

serving suggestion Serve with mixed green salad.

spicy chicken and ratatouille pilaf

2 tablespoons olive oil
1 medium red onion (170g), chopped coarsely
3 cloves garlic, sliced thinly
4 medium tomatoes (600g), chopped coarsely
2 medium zucchini (240g), chopped coarsely
1 medium eggplant (300g), chopped coarsely
1 medium red capsicum (bell pepper) (200g),
  chopped coarsely
1 cup (250g) bottled tomato pasta sauce
500g (1 pound) chicken tenderloins, sliced thinly
1 fresh long red chilli, chopped finely
1 cup (200g) basmati rice
1½ cups (375ml) chicken stock
¼ cup loosely packed fresh basil leaves

1 Preheat oven to 200°C/400°F.
2 Combine all ingredients, except basil, in
2.5-litre (10-cup) ovenproof dish. Cover tightly
with foil; bake about 50 minutes, stirring
occasionally, or until rice is tender.
3 Stand, covered, 10 minutes; season to taste.
Serve sprinkled with basil.

prep + cook time 1 hour 10 minutes serves 4
nutritional count per serving 9g total fat
(1.5g saturated fat); 1430kJ (342cal);
36.9g carbohydrate; 25.2g protein; 5.3g fibre

tip Using a round or oval dish will help the rice to
cook more evenly, square corners attract the heat
from the oven which can cause the rice in the
corners to dry out.

chicken penne carbonara with crispy crumbs

250g (8 ounces) penne pasta
2 teaspoons olive oil
8 slices prosciutto (120g), sliced thinly
2 cloves garlic, crushed
3 cups (480g) shredded barbecued chicken
4 eggs
1 cup (250ml) pouring cream
1 cup (80g) coarsely grated parmesan cheese
¼ cup coarsely chopped fresh chives
1½ cups (105g) coarse stale breadcrumbs

1 Preheat oven to 200°C/400°F.
2 Cook pasta in large saucepan of boiling water until tender; drain.
3 Meanwhile, heat oil in same pan; cook prosciutto, stirring, about 5 minutes or until crisp. Add garlic; cook, stirring, 1 minute. Add pasta to prosciutto mixture with chicken.
4 Whisk eggs, cream, cheese and chives in large jug; season, stir into pasta mixture.
5 Spoon mixture into 2-litre (8-cup) ovenproof dish; sprinkle with breadcrumbs. Bake, uncovered, about 25 minutes or until browned lightly.

prep + cook time 45 minutes **serves** 4
nutritional count per serving 55.2g total fat (27.9g saturated fat); 4238kJ (1014cal); 62.8g carbohydrate; 64.8g protein; 4.8g fibre

serving suggestion Serve with mixed green salad.

tips You need to purchase a large barbecued chicken to provide the amount of shredded meat required for this recipe. For the breadcrumbs, we used ciabatta with crust left on, cut into pieces then processed.

chicken, noodle and asparagus frittata

350g (11 ounces) fresh singapore noodles
1 tablespoon peanut oil
300g (9½ ounces) chicken tenderloins,
  sliced thinly
175g (5½ ounces) asparagus, trimmed,
  chopped coarsely
2 cloves garlic, crushed
2.5cm (1-inch) piece fresh ginger (15g), grated
2 green onions (scallions), sliced thinly
8 eggs
1 cup (80g) bean sprouts
30g (1 ounce) snow pea sprouts
2 tablespoons kecap manis

1 Preheat oven to 220°C/ 425°F.
2 Place noodles in large heatproof bowl; cover
with boiling water, stand until tender. Rinse under
cold water; drain.
3 Heat oil in 25cm (10-inch) ovenproof frying pan;
cook chicken until browned. Add asparagus; cook,
stirring, until tender. Add garlic, ginger and onion;
cook, stirring, about 1 minute or until fragrant.
Cool 5 minutes.
4 Whisk eggs in large bowl; stir in noodles and
asparagus mixture. Season. Carefully pour mixture
into same cleaned, oiled pan. Cover with foil; bake
15 minutes. Uncover; bake about 10 minutes or
until set. Serve frittata topped with combined
sprouts; drizzle with kecap manis.

prep + cook time 35 minutes serves 4
nutritional count per serving 17.4g total fat
(4.6g saturated fat); 2174kJ (520cal);
47.7g carbohydrate; 41g protein; 3.6g fibre

chicken stroganoff with potato topping

4 medium potatoes (800g), chopped coarsely
½ cup (125ml) milk
60g (2 ounces) butter
500g (1 pound) chicken thigh fillets, sliced thinly
¼ cup (35g) plain (all-purpose) flour
2 tablespoons olive oil
45g (1½ ounces) butter, extra
1 large brown onion (200g), sliced thinly
2 cloves garlic, crushed
185g (6 ounces) button mushrooms, sliced thinly
2 teaspoons sweet paprika
⅓ cup (80ml) dry white wine
1 cup (250ml) chicken stock
1 tablespoon worcestershire sauce
¼ cup (70g) tomato paste
½ cup (120g) light sour cream
2 tablespoons finely chopped fresh
   flat-leaf parsley

1 Preheat oven to 220°C/425°F.
2 Boil, steam or microwave potato until tender; drain. Mash potato with milk and butter in large bowl until smooth.
3 Meanwhile, coat chicken in flour; shake off excess. Heat oil in large saucepan; cook chicken until browned. Remove from pan.
4 Melt extra butter in same pan; cook onion, garlic and mushrooms, stirring, until vegetables soften. Add paprika; cook, stirring, about 1 minute or until fragrant. Add wine and stock; simmer, uncovered, until liquid is reduced by half. Return chicken to pan with sauce, paste and sour cream; bring to the boil. Remove from heat; stir in parsley. Season to taste.
5 Spoon chicken mixture into 2.5-litre (10-cup) ovenproof dish. Top with potato; roughen surface with a fork. Bake, uncovered, about 30 minutes or until browned lightly.

prep + cook time 1 hour serves 6
nutritional count per serving 31.7g total fat (15.4g saturated fat); 2052kJ (491cal); 24.9g carbohydrate; 22.8g protein; 3.9g fibre

chicken biryani with cauliflower and peas

¼ cup (70g) yogurt
2 cups (540g) bottled butter chicken
    simmer sauce
500g (1 pound) chicken thigh fillets, trimmed,
    chopped coarsely
1½ cups (300g) basmati rice
2 tablespoons vegetable oil
2½ cups (250g) cauliflower florets
1 large brown onion (200g), sliced thinly
3 cloves garlic, crushed
2.5cm (1-inch) piece fresh ginger (15g), grated
1 fresh long green chilli, sliced thinly
1 tablespoon garam masala
4 cloves
2 teaspoons ground turmeric
3 cups (750ml) chicken stock
½ cup (60g) frozen peas, thawed
⅓ cup (55g) dried currants
¼ cup loosely packed fresh coriander
    (cilantro) leaves

1 Combine yogurt, ¼ cup of the simmer sauce and chicken in large bowl. Cover; refrigerate 1 hour.
2 Preheat oven to 200°C/400°F.
3 Rinse rice under cold water until water runs clear; drain. Heat half the oil in large flameproof casserole dish; cook cauliflower, stirring, about 5 minutes or until browned lightly and tender. Remove from pan.
4 Heat remaining oil in same dish; cook onion, stirring, until browned lightly. Add chicken; cook, stirring, until browned. Add garlic, ginger, chilli and spices; cook, stirring, about 1 minute or until fragrant. Add rice; cook, stirring, 1 minute. Stir in stock. Cover; bake about 45 minutes or until rice is tender and liquid absorbed.
5 Remove dish from oven; add cauliflower, peas and currants. Cover, stand for 10 minutes. Fluff rice with a fork; season to taste.
6 Bring remaining simmer sauce to the boil in small saucepan. Serve biryani topped with heated simmer sauce, coriander leaves and some extra yogurt, if you like.

prep + cook time 1 hour 15 minutes (+ refrigeration)
serves 4
nutritional count per serving 32.1g total fat
(9.9g saturated fat); 3260kJ (780 cal);
84.7g carbohydrate; 35.1g protein; 7.5g fibre

red wine and rosemary chicken with polenta crust

8 chicken thigh fillets (1.6kg), halved
2 tablespoons plain (all-purpose) flour
1 teaspoon cracked black pepper
2 tablespoons olive oil
125g (4 ounces) speck, chopped coarsely
8 shallots (200g), halved
1 large carrot (180g), chopped coarsely
4 cloves garlic, sliced thinly
2 sprigs rosemary
1 cup (250ml) dry red wine
1 cup (250ml) chicken stock
2 tablespoons tomato paste
½ cup (50g) coarsely grated mozzarella cheese

POLENTA CRUST
1 cup (250ml) chicken stock
1 cup (250ml) milk
½ cup (85g) polenta

1 Preheat oven to 200°C/400°F.
2 Coat chicken in combined flour and pepper; shake off excess.
3 Heat oil in large frying pan; cook chicken, in batches, until browned. Remove from pan.
4 Cook speck, shallots, carrot and garlic in same pan, stirring, until browned lightly. Return chicken to pan with rosemary, wine, stock and paste; bring to the boil. Season. Spoon mixture into six 1-cup (250ml) ovenproof dishes; bake, covered, 20 minutes.
5 Meanwhile, make polenta crust.
6 Spread polenta crust mixture over chicken mixture; sprinkle with cheese. Bake, uncovered, about 20 minutes or until browned lightly. Stand 10 minutes before serving.

POLENTA CRUST Bring stock and milk to the boil in small saucepan; gradually stir in polenta. Reduce heat; simmer, stirring, about 10 minutes or until polenta thickens.

prep + cook time 1 hour 40 minutes serves 6
nutritional count per serving 34.7g total fat (11.9g saturated fat); 2972kJ (711cal); 30.4g carbohydrate; 61.5g protein; 2.6g fibre

tip If speck is unavailable, use three chopped bacon slices.

meat

pork sausage cassoulet

2 teaspoons olive oil
8 thick pork sausages (960g)
1 large brown onion (200g), chopped finely
155g (5 ounces) piece pancetta, chopped finely
1 medium carrot (120g), chopped coarsely
1 stalk celery (150g), trimmed, chopped coarsely
2 cloves garlic, crushed
2 tablespoons tomato paste
1½ cups (375ml) chicken stock
410g (13 ounces) canned crushed tomatoes
1 teaspoon fennel seeds
400g (12½ ounces) canned white beans,
  rinsed, drained
2 thick slices (100g) sourdough bread
1 tablespoon coarsely chopped fresh
  flat-leaf parsley

1 Preheat oven to 200°C/400°F.
2 Heat oil in large flameproof casserole dish; cook sausages, until browned. Drain sausages on absorbent paper, chop coarsely.
3 Cook onion, pancetta, carrot, celery and garlic in same dish, stirring, until onion softens. Add paste; cook, stirring, 1 minute. Return sausages to dish with stock, undrained tomatoes, fennel seeds and beans; bring to the boil. Bake, uncovered, 30 minutes.
4 Preheat grill (broiler). Season cassoulet to taste. Top with chunks of sourdough; grill until browned lightly. Sprinkle with parsley.

prep + cook time 1 hour 10 minutes serves 6
nutritional count per serving 41.6g total fat
(16.2g saturated fat); 2416kJ (578 cal);
20.2g carbohydrate; 28.8g protein; 6.2g fibre

lamb shank shepherd's pie

4 french-trimmed lamb shanks (1kg)
⅓ cup (50g) plain (all-purpose) flour
2 tablespoons olive oil
8 baby brown onions (200g), peeled
1 large carrot (180g), chopped coarsely
4 cloves garlic, sliced thinly
2 tablespoons each fresh thyme and
   rosemary leaves
½ cup (125ml) dry white wine
1¼ cups (310ml) chicken stock
1¼ cups (310ml) water
1kg (2 pounds) potatoes, chopped coarsely
45g (1½ ounces) butter
½ cup (125ml) hot milk

CREAMED SPINACH
1 tablespoon olive oil
30g (1 ounce) butter
1 small brown onion (80g), chopped finely
2 cloves garlic, crushed
1kg (2 pounds) spinach, trimmed
½ cup (125ml) pouring cream
pinch ground nutmeg

1 Preheat oven to 200°C/400°F.
2 Coat lamb in flour; shake off excess. Heat half the oil in large flameproof casserole dish; cook lamb until browned. Remove from dish.
3 Heat remaining oil in same dish; cook onions, carrot, garlic and herbs, stirring, until onions are browned lightly. Add wine; boil, uncovered, until liquid is evaporated. Return lamb to dish with stock and the water; bring to the boil. Cover dish tightly with foil; bake about 2 hours or until lamb is tender.
4 Meanwhile, boil, steam or microwave potato until tender; drain. Mash potato in medium bowl with butter and hot milk until smooth. Season to taste. Make creamed spinach.
5 Remove dish from oven; discard lamb shank bones. Break meat into large chunks; return meat to dish. Combine potato and spinach in large bowl; spoon over lamb mixture. Bake, uncovered, about 30 minutes or until browned lightly.

CREAMED SPINACH Heat oil and butter in large frying pan; cook onion and garlic, stirring, until onion softens. Add spinach, in batches, stirring, until wilted and liquid is evaporated. Add cream and nutmeg; simmer about 3 minutes or until thickened slightly. Season to taste.

prep + cook time 2 hours 50 minutes serves 6
nutritional count per serving 38.4g total fat (18.4g saturated fat); 2575kJ (616 cal); 30.8g carbohydrate; 29.5g protein; 8.8g fibre

beef stew with chive dumplings

1kg (2 pounds) beef chuck steak,
  chopped coarsely
2 tablespoons plain (all-purpose) flour
2 tablespoons olive oil
15g (½ ounce) butter
1 medium brown onion (150g), chopped coarsely
2 cloves garlic, crushed
1 medium parsnip (250g), chopped coarsely
1 medium carrot (120g), chopped coarsely
1 cup (250ml) dry red wine
1½ cups (375ml) beef stock
2 tablespoons tomato paste
4 sprigs fresh thyme

CHIVE DUMPLINGS
1 cup (150g) self-raising flour
60g (2 ounces) butter, chopped finely
1 egg, beaten lightly
¼ cup (20g) coarsely grated parmesan cheese
¼ cup finely chopped fresh chives
¼ cup (60ml) milk, approximately

1 Preheat oven to 180°C/350°F.
2 Coat beef in flour; shake off excess. Heat oil in large flameproof baking dish; cook beef, in batches, until browned. Remove from dish.
3 Melt butter in same dish; cook onion, garlic, parsnip and carrot, stirring, until onion softens. Add wine; cook, stirring, until liquid reduces by half. Return beef to dish with stock, paste and thyme; bring to the boil. Season. Cover; bake 1¾ hours.
4 Meanwhile, make chive dumplings.
5 Remove dish from oven. Drop rounded tablespoons of dumpling mixture, about 2cm (¾ inch) apart, on top of stew. Bake, uncovered, about 25 minutes or until dumplings are browned lightly.

CHIVE DUMPLINGS Place flour in medium bowl; rub in butter. Stir in egg, cheese, chives and enough milk to make a soft sticky dough.

prep + cook time 2 hours 20 minutes serves 4
nutritional count per serving 47.7g total fat (19.7g saturated fat); 3837kJ (918 cal); 42.3g carbohydrate; 67.5g protein; 5.1g fibre

baked meatballs

1kg (2 pounds) minced (ground) beef
2 eggs
1 cup (100g) packaged breadcrumbs
½ cup (40g) finely grated parmesan cheese
⅓ cup finely chopped fresh flat-leaf parsley
¼ cup (60ml) olive oil
1 medium brown onion (150g), chopped finely
2 cloves garlic, crushed
2⅔ cups (700g) bottled tomato pasta sauce
800g (1½ pounds) canned crushed tomatoes
1 cup (120g) frozen peas
½ cup coarsely chopped fresh basil
200g (6½ ounces) ricotta cheese
½ cup (40g) finely grated parmesan cheese, extra

1 Preheat oven to 200°C/400°F. Oil 3-litre (12-cup) ovenproof dish.
2 Combine beef, eggs, breadcrumbs, parmesan and parsley in large bowl; season. Using wet hands, roll rounded tablespoons of mixture into balls.
3 Heat half the oil in large frying pan; cook meatballs, in batches, until browned all over. Transfer to dish.
4 Heat remaining oil in same pan; cook onion and garlic, stirring, until onion softens. Remove from heat; stir in sauce, undrained tomatoes, peas and basil; season. Pour tomato mixture over meatballs; top with crumbled ricotta and extra parmesan. Bake, uncovered, about 40 minutes or until meatballs are cooked through.

prep + cook time 1 hour 10 minutes serves 6
nutritional count per serving 34.3g total fat (13.4g saturated fat); 2642kJ (632 cal); 27.3g carbohydrate; 50.9g protein; 7.1g fibre

serving suggestion Serve with pasta or crusty bread and a green salad.

osso bucco with polenta crust

8 pieces veal osso bucco (1.4kg)
⅓ cup (50g) plain (all-purpose) flour
2 tablespoons olive oil
30g (1 ounce) butter
1 large brown onion (200g), chopped finely
1 large carrot (180g), chopped finely
1 stalk celery (150g), chopped finely
4 cloves garlic, crushed
½ cup (125ml) dry white wine
800g (1½ pounds) canned crushed tomatoes
2 sprigs fresh rosemary
1 cup (250ml) chicken stock
1 tablespoon finely chopped fresh flat-leaf parsley
2 teaspoons finely grated lemon rind

POLENTA CRUST
2 cups (500ml) milk
2 cups (500ml) water
1 cup (150g) instant polenta
½ cup (40g) finely grated parmesan cheese
1 egg, beaten lightly

1 Preheat oven to 200°C/400°F.
2 Coat veal in flour; shake off excess. Heat half the oil and butter in large flameproof baking dish; cook veal, in batches, until browned. Remove from dish.
3 Heat remaining oil and butter in same dish; cook onion, carrot, celery and garlic, stirring, until onion softens. Add wine; boil, uncovered, until liquid has evaporated. Return veal to dish with undrained tomatoes, rosemary and stock; bring to the boil. Season. Cover tightly with foil; bake 1½ hours.
4 Meanwhile, make polenta crust.
5 Remove dish from oven; discard veal bones and rosemary. Break meat into large chunks. Divide veal mixture among eight oiled 1¼-cup (310ml) ovenproof dishes; top with polenta crust mixture. Place dishes on oven tray; bake, uncovered, about 25 minutes or until browned lightly. Serve sprinkled with combined parsley and rind.

POLENTA CRUST Combine milk and the water in medium saucepan; bring almost to the boil. Gradually stir in polenta, cook, stirring, about 5 minutes or until thickened. Remove from heat, stir in cheese and egg; season to taste.

prep + cook time 2 hours 20 minutes serves 8
nutritional count per serving 15.3g total fat (6.3g saturated fat); 1705kJ (408 cal); 26.7g carbohydrate; 36.5g protein; 3.4g fibre

note We used larger dishes here – each dish will serve four.

salami antipasto pasta

375g (12 ounces) large shell pasta
200g (6½ ounces) shaved salami,
  chopped coarsely
⅓ cup (20g) drained semi-dried tomatoes
280g (9 ounces) bottled char-grilled vegetables,
  drained, chopped coarsely
2⅔ cups (700g) bottled tomato pasta sauce
2 cups (500ml) water
⅓ cup each coarsely chopped fresh basil and
  flat-leaf parsley
1 cup (100g) coarsely grated mozzarella cheese

1 Preheat oven to 200°C/400°F. Oil 2.5-litre
(10-cup) baking dish.
2 Combine pasta, salami, tomatoes, vegetables,
sauce, the water and chopped herbs in dish;
season lightly.
3 Cover dish with foil; bake 50 minutes, stirring
halfway through cooking. Remove from oven;
sprinkle with cheese. Bake, uncovered, about
20 minutes or until pasta is tender.

prep + cook time 1 hour 20 minutes **serves** 6
nutritional count per serving 19.5g total fat
(6.8g saturated fat); 2098kJ (502 cal);
57.5g carbohydrate; 21.3g protein; 5.7g fibre

tip We have deliberately used dried, uncooked
pasta in this dish. The texture of the final dish is
a little chewy, but still tender.
note We cooked this recipe in two ovenproof
dishes – each dish will serve three.

chorizo and chickpea stew

2 tablespoons olive oil
2 cured chorizo sausages (340g), sliced thickly
2 medium brown onions (300g), sliced thinly
1 tablespoon light brown sugar
2 teaspoons cumin seeds
1 teaspoon ground coriander
800g (1½ pounds) canned crushed tomatoes
800g (1½ pounds) canned chickpeas (garbanzos)
  rinsed, drained
1 cup (250ml) salt-reduced chicken stock
½ cup (75g) raisins
60g (2 ounces) baby spinach leaves

1 Preheat oven to 200°C/400°F.
2 Heat half the oil in large baking dish; cook chorizo, stirring, until browned. Remove from dish. Add onion and sugar to same dish; cook, stirring occasionally, over medium heat, about 15 minutes or until onion is lightly caramelised. Add spices; cook, stirring, 1 minute.
3 Return chorizo to dish with undrained tomatoes, chickpeas, stock and raisins; bring to the boil. Cover; bake 40 minutes. Remove from oven; stir in spinach. Season to taste.

prep and cook time 1 hour 10 minutes **serves** 6
nutritional count per serving 25.5g total fat
(7.4g saturated fat); 1852kJ (443 cal);
31.8g carbohydrate; 19.3g protein; 7.5g fibre

rich beef mince pie

1½ cups (225g) plain (all-purpose) flour
90g (3 ounces) butter, chopped finely
1 egg
1 tablespoon iced water, approximately
2 sheets puff pastry
1 egg, beaten lightly, extra

BEEF FILLING
1 tablespoon olive oil
1 medium brown onion (150g), chopped finely
625g (1¼ pounds) minced (ground) beef
410g (13 ounces) canned diced tomatoes
¾ cup (180ml) beef stock
¼ cup (60ml) worcestershire sauce
2 tablespoons tomato paste
2 tablespoons cornflour (cornstarch)
2 tablespoons water

1 Process flour and butter until crumbly. Add egg and enough of the water to make ingredients come together. Knead on floured surface until smooth. Cover; refrigerate 30 minutes.
2 Preheat oven to 200°C/400°F. Oil deep 24cm (9½-inch) pie dish.
3 Roll dough between sheets of baking paper until large enough to line dish. Lift pastry into dish, ease into side; trim edges. Place dish on oven tray; lightly prick base with fork. Line with baking paper and fill with dried beans or rice; bake 10 minutes. Remove paper and beans; bake 10 minutes or until browned lightly. Cool.
4 Meanwhile, make beef filling.
5 Spoon beef filling into pastry case; brush edges with extra egg. Place one puff pastry sheet on top of the other; using rolling pin, roll pastry until large enough to cover filling. Lift pastry over filling; press edges together using fork to seal, trim excess, brush with egg. Bake about 20 minutes or until browned. Stand 5 minutes before serving.

BEEF FILLING Heat oil in medium saucepan; cook onion, stirring, until soft. Add beef; cook, stirring, until browned. Add undrained tomatoes, stock, sauce and paste; bring to the boil. Reduce heat; simmer, uncovered, 20 minutes. Add blended cornflour and the water; cook, stirring, until mixture boils and thickens. Season to taste; cool.

prep + cook time 1 hour 40 minutes
(+ refrigeration and standing) serves 6
nutritional count per serving 38.3g total fat
(13.9g saturated fat); 2943kJ (704 cal);
56.7g carbohydrate; 31.8g protein; 3.7g fibre

veal goulash with parsley dumplings

2 tablespoons olive oil
45g (1½ ounces) butter
1kg (2 pounds) veal shoulder, chopped coarsely
1 large red capsicum (bell pepper) (350g),
  chopped coarsely
1 large brown onion (200g), chopped coarsely
2 cloves garlic, crushed
2 tablespoons tomato paste
1 tablespoon plain (all-purpose) flour
1 tablespoon sweet paprika
2 teaspoons caraway seeds
½ teaspoon cayenne pepper
1½ cups (375ml) beef stock
½ cup (125ml) water
2 tablespoons coarsely chopped fresh
  flat-leaf parsley
¼ cup (20g) finely grated parmesan cheese

PARSLEY DUMPLINGS
1 cup (150g) self-raising flour
60g (2 ounces) butter, chopped finely
1 egg, beaten lightly
⅓ cup finely chopped fresh flat-leaf parsley
¼ cup (20g) finely grated parmesan cheese
¼ cup (60ml) milk, approximately

1 Preheat oven to 180°C/350°F.
2 Heat half the oil and butter in large flameproof casserole dish; cook veal, in batches, until browned. Remove from dish.
3 Heat remaining oil and butter in same dish; cook capsicum, onion and garlic, stirring, until vegetables soften. Add paste, flour, paprika, caraway and cayenne; cook, stirring, 1 minute. Return veal to dish with stock and the water; bring to the boil. Cover; bake 1½ hours.
4 Meanwhile, make parsley dumplings.
5 Remove dish from oven; stir in parsley. Season to taste. Drop rounded tablespoons of the dumpling mixture, about 2cm (¾ inch) apart, on top of goulash; sprinkle dumplings with cheese. Bake, uncovered, about 20 minutes or until dumplings are cooked through.

PARSLEY DUMPLINGS Place flour in medium bowl; rub in butter. Stir in egg, parsley, cheese and enough milk to make a soft sticky dough.

prep + cook time 2 hours 20 minutes serves 4
nutritional count per serving 42.7g total fat (20.2g saturated fat); 3344kJ (800 cal); 35.7g carbohydrate; 67g protein; 3.7g fibre

egg and bacon pie

5 sheets fillo pastry
45g (1½ ounces) butter, melted
4 rindless bacon slices (260g), chopped finely
6 eggs
⅔ cup (160ml) milk
¾ cup (90g) coarsely grated cheddar cheese

1 Preheat oven to 200°C/400°F. Oil 20cm (8-inch) springform tin; place on oven tray.
2 Brush one sheet of fillo pastry with some of the melted butter; fold in half, then ease into base and side of tin. Repeat with remaining pastry and melted butter, to completely cover base and side of tin.
3 Cook bacon in heated oiled frying pan until crisp; drain on absorbent paper. Combine eggs and milk in large jug; season.
4 Place bacon and half the cheese in tin; pour in egg mixture. Sprinkle with remaining cheese. Roll down edges of pastry until touching egg mixture; bake, uncovered, about 45 minutes or until set. Stand 10 minutes before serving.

prep + cook time 1 hour 10 minutes serves 4
nutritional count per serving 32.5g total fat (16.6g saturated fat); 1965kJ (470 cal); 12.4g carbohydrate; 32.5g protein; 0.7g fibre

sausage risotto

1 tablespoon olive oil
6 thick beef sausages (900g)
1 medium brown onion (150g), chopped finely
¼ cup firmly packed fresh basil leaves
2 cloves garlic, crushed
2 cups (400g) arborio rice
2 tablespoons tomato paste
½ cup (125ml) dry white wine
2⅔ cups (700g) bottled tomato pasta sauce
2½ cups (625ml) water
2 teaspoons caster (superfine) sugar
60g (2 ounces) baby rocket (arugula) leaves

1   Preheat oven to 180°C/350°F.
2   Heat oil in large flameproof casserole dish;
cook sausages, in batches, until browned.
Remove from dish; cut into thirds.
3   Cook onion, basil and garlic in same dish,
stirring, until onion softens. Add rice and paste;
stir to coat rice in onion mixture. Add wine; bring
to the boil. Boil, uncovered, stirring until liquid is
absorbed. Stir in sauce, the water and sugar;
bring to the boil. Season.
4   Cover dish with foil; bake 25 minutes, stirring
halfway through cooking. Uncover; stir in sausages.
Bake about 10 minutes or until rice is tender.
Stir in rocket.

prep + cook time 1 hour serves 6
nutritional count per serving 43.5g total fat
(18.9g saturated fat); 3298kJ (789 cal);
68.7g carbohydrate; 24.6g protein; 8g fibre

beef ragu cannelloni

2 tablespoons olive oil
1 stalk celery (150g), trimmed, chopped finely
1 small brown onion (80g), chopped finely
1 small carrot (80g), chopped finely
2 fresh long red chillies, chopped finely
1 clove garlic, crushed
45g (1½-ounce) piece pancetta, chopped finely
250g (8 ounces) minced (ground) beef
200g (6½ ounces) minced (ground) pork
⅓ cup (80ml) dry white wine
¾ cup (180ml) milk
1 cup (250ml) chicken stock
410g (13 ounces) canned diced tomatoes
2 tablespoons tomato paste
2⅓ cups (580ml) thickened (heavy) cream
¾ cup (60g) finely grated parmesan cheese
250g (8 ounces) fresh cannelloni sheets

1 Heat half the oil in medium saucepan; cook celery, onion, carrot, chilli and garlic, stirring, until onion softens. Add pancetta; cook, stirring, 3 minutes. Remove from pan.
2 Heat remaining oil in same pan; cook beef and pork, stirring, until browned. Return pancetta mixture to pan with wine; boil, uncovered, until reduced by half. Add milk; bring to the boil. Boil, uncovered, until reduced by half. Add stock, undrained tomatoes and paste; bring to the boil. Reduce heat; simmer, uncovered, about 1 hour 10 minutes or until thickened. Season to taste. Cool 20 minutes.
3 Preheat oven to 200°C/400°F. Oil shallow 3.5-litre (14-cup) ovenproof dish.
4 Combine cream and cheese in large jug; season. Spread 1 cup (250ml) of the cream mixture over base of dish.
5 Carefully tear each cannelloni sheet into three pieces. Place ¼ cup of beef mixture along one short side of each piece; roll to enclose. Place cannelloni, seam-side down, into dish; pour remaining cream mixture over cannelloni. Cover with foil; bake 30 minutes. Uncover; bake about 15 minutes or until browned lightly. Stand 5 minutes before serving.

prep + cook time 2 hours 15 minutes (+ cooling)
serves 6
nutritional count per serving 54.3g total fat (30.3g saturated fat); 3097kJ (741 cal); 31.7g carbohydrate; 28.9g protein; 3.4g fibre

sweet and sour meatballs

1kg (2 pounds) minced (ground) beef
2 eggs
1 cup (100g) packaged breadcrumbs
1 tablespoon finely chopped fresh flat-leaf parsley
¼ cup (60ml) olive oil
1 large red capsicum (bell pepper) (350g),
  chopped coarsely
1 large brown onion (200g), chopped coarsely
1 large carrot (180g), chopped coarsely
2 stalks celery (300g), trimmed, chopped coarsely

SWEET AND SOUR SAUCE
440g (14 ounces) canned pineapple pieces
  in natural juice
2 tablespoons cornflour (cornstarch)
2 tablespoons light soy sauce
¾ cup (180ml) water
⅔ cup (160ml) white vinegar
⅓ cup (80ml) tomato sauce (ketchup)
3 teaspoons caster (superfine) sugar

1 Preheat oven to 200°C/400°F. Oil 3-litre
(12-cup) ovenproof dish.
2 Make sweet and sour sauce.
3 Combine beef, eggs, breadcrumbs and parsley
in large bowl; season. Using wet hands, roll
rounded tablespoons of beef mixture into balls.
4 Heat half the oil in large frying pan; cook
meatballs, in batches, until browned. Transfer
to dish. Heat remaining oil in same pan; cook
capsicum, onion, carrot and celery, stirring, until
onion softens. Add sweet and sour sauce; bring
to the boil. Remove from heat; stir in reserved
pineapple pieces.
5 Pour vegetable mixture over meatballs
in dish. Cover dish with foil; bake 30 minutes.
Uncover; bake about 10 minutes or until
meatballs are cooked.

SWEET AND SOUR SAUCE Drain pineapple
through sieve into large jug; reserve juice. Blend
cornflour with soy sauce in medium jug; add juice,
the water, vinegar, tomato sauce and sugar. Season.

prep + cook time 1 hour serves 6
nutritional count per serving 24.1g total fat
(8.1g saturated fat); 2149kJ (514 cal);
31.9g carbohydrate; 39.8g protein; 3.9g fibre

serving suggestion Serve with steamed
jasmine rice.

lamb and eggplant pot pies with fetta crust

2 tablespoons olive oil
1 large eggplant (450g), peeled, chopped coarsely
1 large brown onion (200g), chopped finely
4 cloves garlic, crushed
1kg (2 pounds) minced (ground) lamb
1 teaspoon ground cinnamon
½ teaspoon ground allspice
1½ cups (375ml) beef stock
2 tablespoons tomato paste
¼ cup (20g) finely grated parmesan cheese
2 tablespoons each finely chopped fresh mint
  and oregano

FETTA CRUST
750g (1½ pounds) potatoes, chopped coarsely
30g (1 ounce) butter
¼ cup (60ml) hot milk
200g (6½ ounces) fetta cheese, crumbled

1 Heat half the oil in large saucepan; cook eggplant, stirring, until tender. Remove from pan. Heat remaining oil in same pan; cook onion and garlic, stirring, until onion softens. Add lamb; cook, stirring, until browned. Add spices; cook, stirring, 1 minute. Add stock and paste; bring to the boil. Reduce heat; simmer, uncovered, about 20 minutes or until thickened slightly. Remove from heat; stir in parmesan, herbs and eggplant.
2 Meanwhile, make fetta crust.
3 Preheat oven to 200°C/400°F. Oil six 1-cup (250ml) ovenproof dishes; place on oven trays.
4 Divide lamb mixture among dishes; top with fetta crust. Bake, uncovered, about 30 minutes or until browned lightly.

FETTA CRUST Boil, steam or microwave potato until tender; drain. Mash potato in medium bowl with butter and milk until smooth. Stir in fetta; season to taste.

prep and cook time 1 hour 10 minutes serves 6
nutritional count per serving 32.3g total fat (15.3g saturated fat); 2341kJ (560 cal); 19g carbohydrate; 46.4g protein; 4.5g fibre

glossary

ALLSPICE also called pimento or jamaican pepper; tastes like a combination of nutmeg, cumin, clove and cinnamon. Sold whole or ground.

BAKING PAPER also known as parchment paper or baking parchment – is a silicone-coated paper that is primarily used for lining baking pans and oven trays so cakes and biscuits won't stick, making removal easy.

BALSAMIC VINEGAR originally from Modena, Italy, there are now many varieties on the market.

BEAN SPROUTS tender new growths of assorted beans and seeds germinated for consumption as sprouts.

BEANS

broad also called fava, windsor and horse beans; available dried, fresh, canned and frozen. Fresh should be peeled twice (discarding both the outer long green pod and the beige-green tough inner shell); the frozen beans have had their pods removed but the beige shell still needs removal.

kidney medium-size red bean, slightly floury in texture yet sweet in flavour; sold dried or canned, it's found in bean mixes and is used in chilli con carne.

white a generic term we use for canned or dried cannellini, haricot, navy or great northern beans belonging to the same family, phaseolus vulgaris.

BREADCRUMBS

fresh bread, usually white, processed into crumbs.

japanese also called panko; available in two kinds: larger pieces and fine crumbs; they have a lighter texture than Western-style breadcrumbs. Available from Asian food stores and some supermarkets.

packaged prepared fine-textured but crunchy white breadcrumbs; good for coating foods that are to be fried.

stale crumbs made by grating or processing one- or two-day-old bread.

CAPERS the grey-green buds of a warm climate (usually Mediterranean) shrub, sold either dried and salted or pickled in a vinegar brine; tiny young ones, called baby capers, are also available both in brine or dried in salt. Their pungent taste adds piquancy.

CAPSICUM also called pepper or bell pepper. Discard seeds and membranes before use.

CARAWAY SEEDS the small, half-moon-shaped dried seed from a member of the parsley family; adds a sharp anise flavour when used in both sweet and savoury dishes.

CAYENNE PEPPER a thin-fleshed, long, extremely hot dried red chilli, usually purchased ground.

CHEESE

blue mould-treated cheeses mottled with blue veining. Varieties include firm and crumbly stilton types and mild, creamy brie-like cheeses.

cheddar semi-hard, yellow to off-white, sharp-tasting cheese named after the village in Somerset, England in which it was originally produced.

fetta Greek in origin; a crumbly textured goat- or sheep-milk cheese having a sharp, salty taste. Ripened and stored in salted whey; particularly good cubed and tossed into salads.

gorgonzola a creamy Italian blue cheese with a mild, sweet taste; good as an accompaniment to fruit or used to flavour sauces (especially pasta).

gruyère a hard-rind Swiss cheese with small holes and a nutty, slightly salty flavour. Popular for soufflés.

mozzarella soft, spun-curd cheese; originating in southern Italy where it was traditionally made from water-buffalo milk. Now generally made from cow's milk, it's a popular pizza cheese because of its low melting point and elasticity when heated.

parmesan also called parmigiano; is a hard, grainy cow's-milk cheese originating in the Parma region of Italy. The curd for this cheese is salted in brine for a month, then aged for up to two years in humid conditions. Reggiano is the best parmesan variety, aged for a minimum two years and made only in the northern Italian region of Emilia-Romagna.

pizza cheese a commercial blend of varying proportions of processed grated mozzarella, cheddar and parmesan.

ricotta a soft, sweet, moist, white cow's-milk cheese with a low fat content (8.5 per cent) and a slightly grainy texture. The name roughly translates as "cooked again" and refers to ricotta's manufacture from a whey that is itself a by-product of cheese making.

CHICKPEAS also called garbanzos, hummus or channa; an irregularly round, sandy-coloured legume used extensively in Mediterranean, Indian and Hispanic cooking. Firm texture even after cooking, a floury mouth-feel and robust nutty flavour; available canned or dried (reconstitute for several hours in water before use).

CHIPOLATA SAUSAGES also known as 'little fingers'; highly spiced, coarse-textured beef sausage.

CHORIZO SAUSAGE of Spanish origin, made of coarsely ground pork and highly seasoned with garlic and chilli. They are deeply smoked, very spicy and dry-cured. Also available raw.

COCONUT

cream obtained commercially from the first pressing of the coconut flesh alone, without the addition of water; the second pressing (less rich) is sold as coconut milk.

milk not the liquid found inside the fruit, which is called coconut water, but the diluted liquid from the second pressing of the white flesh of a mature coconut (the first pressing produces coconut cream).

CORIANDER also called cilantro, pak chee or chinese parsley; bright-green-leafed herb with both pungent aroma and taste. Used as an ingredient in a wide variety of cuisines. Coriander seeds are dried and sold either whole or ground, and neither form tastes remotely like the fresh leaf.

CORNFLOUR also known as cornstarch. Available made from corn or wheat (wheaten cornflour gives a lighter texture in cakes); used as a thickening agent in cooking.

CREAM we use fresh cream, also known as pure or pouring cream unless otherwise stated. Has no additves. Minimum fat content 35%.
sour a thick, commercially cultured sour cream with a minimum fat content of 35%; light sour cream has 18.5% fat.
thick (double) a dolloping cream with a minimum fat content of 45%.
thickened (heavy) a whipping cream containing thickener. Minimum fat content 35%.

CUMIN also known as zeera or comino; resembling caraway in size, cumin is the dried seed of a plant related to the parsley family. Its spicy, almost curry-like flavour is essential to the traditional foods of Mexico, India, North Africa and the Middle East. Available dried as seeds or ground.

DIJON MUSTARD also called french mustard. Pale brown, creamy, fairly mild mustard.

DRIED CURRANTS tiny, almost black raisins so-named after a grape variety that originated in Corinth, Greece.

EGGPLANT also called aubergine. Ranging in size from tiny to very large and in colour from pale green to deep purple. Can also be purchased char-grilled, packed in oil, in jars.

EGGS we use large chicken eggs weighing an average of 60g unless stated otherwise in the recipes in this book. If a recipe calls for raw or barely cooked eggs, exercise caution if there is a salmonella problem in your area, particularly in food eaten by children and pregnant women.

FENNEL also called finocchio or anise; a crunchy green vegetable slightly resembling celery that's eaten raw in salads, fried as an accompaniment, or used as an ingredient in soups and sauces. Also the name given to the dried seeds of the plant which have a stronger licorice flavour.

FLOUR
plain also known as all-purpose; unbleached wheat flour is the best for baking: the gluten content ensures a strong dough, producing a light result.
self-raising all-purpose plain or wholemeal flour with baking powder and salt added; make yourself with plain flour sifted with baking powder in the proportion of 1 cup flour to 2 teaspoons baking powder.

GARAM MASALA literally meaning blended spices in its northern Indian place of origin; based on varying proportions of cardamom, cinnamon, cloves, coriander, fennel and cumin, roasted and ground together. Black pepper and chilli can be added.

GREEN ONION also known as scallion or (incorrectly) shallot; an immature onion picked before the bulb has formed, with a long, bright-green edible stalk.

HARISSA a North African paste made from dried red chillies, garlic, olive oil and caraway seeds; can be used as a rub for meat, an ingredient in sauces and dressings, or eaten as a condiment. It is available from Middle Eastern food shops and some supermarkets.

HORSERADISH a vegetable with edible green leaves but mainly grown for its long, pungent white root. Occasionally found fresh in specialty greengrocers and some Asian food shops, but commonly purchased in bottles at the supermarket in two forms: prepared horseradish and horseradish cream. These cannot be substituted one for the other in cooking but both can be used as table condiments. Horseradish cream is a commercially prepared creamy paste consisting of grated horseradish, vinegar, oil and sugar, while prepared horseradish is preserved grated root.

KAFFIR LIME LEAVES also known as bai magrood and looks like two glossy dark green leaves joined end to end, forming a rounded hourglass shape. Sold fresh, dried or frozen, the dried leaves are less potent so double the number if using them as a substitute for fresh; a strip of fresh lime peel may be substituted for each kaffir lime leaf.

KECAP MANIS a dark, thick sweet soy sauce used in most South-East Asian cuisines. Depending on the manufacturer, the sauces's sweetness is derived from the addition of either molasses or palm sugar when brewed.

KUMARA the Polynesian name of an orange-fleshed sweet potato often confused with yam; good baked, boiled, mashed or fried similarly to other potatoes.

LEEKS a member of the onion family, the leek resembles a green onion but is much larger and more subtle in flavour. Tender baby or pencil leeks can be eaten whole with minimal cooking but adult leeks are usually trimmed of most of the green tops then chopped or sliced and cooked as an ingredient in stews, casseroles and soups.

MARINARA MIX a mixture of uncooked, chopped seafood available from fishmarkets and fishmongers.

MUSHROOMS
button small, cultivated white mushrooms with a mild flavour. When a recipe calls for an unspecified type of mushroom, use button.
flat large, flat mushrooms with a rich earthy flavour, ideal for filling and barbecuing. They are sometimes misnamed field mushrooms which are wild mushrooms.
swiss brown also known as roman or cremini. Light to dark brown mushrooms with full-bodied flavour; suited for use in casseroles or being stuffed and baked.

MUSTARD SEEDS
black also known as brown mustard seeds; more pungent than the white variety; used frequently in curries.
white also known as yellow mustard seeds; used ground for mustard powder and in most prepared mustards.

OSSO BUCCO another name used by butchers for veal shin, usually cut into 3cm- to 5cm-thick slices and used in the famous Italian slow-cooked casserole of the same name.

PANCETTA an Italian unsmoked bacon, pork belly cured in salt and spices then rolled into a sausage shape and dried for several weeks.

PAPRIKA ground dried sweet red capsicum (bell pepper); many grades and types are available, including sweet, hot, mild and smoked.

PINE NUTS also known as pignoli; not a nut but a small, cream-coloured kernel from pine cones. Best roasted before use to bring out the flavour.

POLENTA also known as cornmeal; a flour-like cereal made of dried corn (maize). Also the dish made from it.

PRESERVED LEMON whole or quartered salted lemons preserved in a mixture of olive oil and lemon juice and occasionally spices such as cinnamon, clove and coriander. Available from delicatessens and specialty food shops. Use the rind only and rinse well before using.

RAISINS dried sweet grapes (traditionally muscatel grapes).

RED CURRY PASTE probably the most popular thai curry paste; a hot blend of different flavours that complements the richness of pork, duck and seafood, also works well in marinades and sauces.

RICE
arborio small, round grain rice well-suited to absorb a large amount of liquid; the high level of starch makes it especially suitable for risottos, giving the dish its classic creaminess.
basmati a white, fragrant long-grained rice; the grains fluff up beautifully when cooked. It should be washed several times before cooking.
jasmine or thai jasmine, is a long-grained white rice recognised around the world for its perfumed aromatic quality; moist texture and the fact that it clings together after cooking. Jasmine rice is sometimes substituted for basmati rice.

ROCKET also called arugula, rugula and rucola; peppery green leaf eaten raw in salads or used in cooking. Baby rocket is smaller and less peppery.

ROLLED OATS flattened oat grain rolled into flakes and traditionally used for porridge. Instant oats are also available for a speedy breakfast, but use traditional oats for baking.

SHALLOTS also called french shallots, golden shallots or eschalots. Small and elongated, with a brown skin, they grow in tight clusters similar to garlic.

SILVER BEET also known as swiss chard and incorrectly, spinach; has fleshy stalks and large leaves, both of which can be prepared as for spinach.

SMOKED HADDOCK smoked fish with white flesh with a milky smoky flavour; skin orange coloured.

SNOW PEA SPROUTS shoots of the snow pea (mange tout) plant. Available from supermarkets or greengrocers and are usually eaten raw in salads or sandwiches.

SOY SAUCE also known as sieu; made from fermented soybeans. Several variations are available in supermarkets and Asian food stores; we use japanese soy sauce unless indicated otherwise.

SPECK smoked pork.

SPINACH also known as english spinach and incorrectly, silver beet. Baby spinach leaves are best eaten raw in salads; the larger leaves should be added last to soups, stews and stir-fries, and should be cooked until barely wilted.

TACO SEASONING MIX a packaged seasoning meant to duplicate the mild Mexican sauce made from oregano, cumin, chillies and other spices.

TOMATOES
bottled tomato pasta sauce a prepared tomato-based sauce (sometimes called ragu or sugo on the label); comes in varying degrees of thickness and kinds of spicing.
canned whole peeled tomatoes in natural juices; available crushed, chopped or diced, sometimes in unsalted or reduced-salt versions. Use undrained.
cherry also known as tiny tim or tom thumb tomatoes; small and round.
egg also called plum or roma, these are smallish, oval-shaped tomatoes much used in Italian cooking or salads.
paste triple-concentrated tomato puree used to flavour soups, stews, sauces and casseroles.
puree canned pureed tomatoes (not tomato paste); substitute with fresh peeled and pureed tomatoes.
sauce also known as ketchup or catsup; a flavoured condiment made from tomatoes, vinegar and spices.
semi-dried partially dried tomato pieces in olive oil; softer and juicier than sun-dried, these are not a preserve therefore do not keep as long as sun-dried.
sun-dried tomato pieces that have been dried with salt; this dehydrates the tomato and concentrates the flavour. We generally use sun-dried tomatoes packaged in oil, unless otherwise specified.
truss small vine-ripened tomatoes with vine still attached.

TORTILLA thin, round unleavened bread originating in Mexico; can be made at home or purchased frozen, fresh or vacuum-packed. Used to make burritos and tostadas. Two kinds of tortilla are available, one made from wheat flour and the other from corn.

TURMERIC also called kamin; is a rhizome related to galangal and ginger. Must be grated or pounded to release its acrid aroma and pungent flavour. Known for the golden colour it imparts, fresh turmeric can be substituted for the more commonly found dried powder

WORCESTERSHIRE SAUCE thin, dark-brown spicy sauce developed by the British when they were resident in India; used as a seasoning for meat, gravies and cocktails, and as a condiment for savoury dishes.

ZUCCHINI also known as courgette; belongs to the squash family. Yellow flowers can be stuffed and deep-fried or used in salads.

conversion chart

MEASURES

One Australian metric measuring cup holds approximately 250ml; one Australian metric tablespoon holds 20ml; one Australian metric teaspoon holds 5ml.

The difference between one country's measuring cups and another's is within a two- or three-teaspoon variance, and will not affect your cooking results. North America, New Zealand and the United Kingdom use a 15ml tablespoon.

All cup and spoon measurements are level. The most accurate way of measuring dry ingredients is to weigh them. When measuring liquids, use a clear glass or plastic jug with the metric markings.

We use large eggs with an average weight of 60g.

DRY MEASURES

METRIC	IMPERIAL
15g	½oz
30g	1oz
60g	2oz
90g	3oz
125g	4oz (¼lb)
155g	5oz
185g	6oz
220g	7oz
250g	8oz (½lb)
280g	9oz
315g	10oz
345g	11oz
375g	12oz (¾lb)
410g	13oz
440g	14oz
470g	15oz
500g	16oz (1lb)
750g	24oz (1½lb)
1kg	32oz (2lb)

LIQUID MEASURES

METRIC	IMPERIAL
30ml	1 fluid oz
60ml	2 fluid oz
100ml	3 fluid oz
125ml	4 fluid oz
150ml	5 fluid oz
190ml	6 fluid oz
250ml	8 fluid oz
300ml	10 fluid oz
500ml	16 fluid oz
600ml	20 fluid oz
1000ml (1 litre)	1¾ pints

LENGTH MEASURES

METRIC	IMPERIAL
3mm	⅛in
6mm	¼in
1cm	½in
2cm	¾in
2.5cm	1in
5cm	2in
6cm	2½in
8cm	3in
10cm	4in
13cm	5in
15cm	6in
18cm	7in
20cm	8in
22cm	9in
25cm	10in
28cm	11in
30cm	12in (1ft)

OVEN TEMPERATURES

The oven temperatures in this book are for conventional ovens; if you have a fan-forced oven, decrease the temperature by 10-20 degrees.

	°C (CELSIUS)	°F (FAHRENHEIT)
Very slow	120	250
Slow	150	300
Moderately slow	160	325
Moderate	180	350
Moderately hot	200	400
Hot	220	425
Very hot	240	475

The imperial measurements used in these recipes are approximate only. Measurements for cake pans are approximate only. Using same-shaped cake pans of a similar size should not affect the outcome of your baking. We measure the inside top of the cake pan to determine sizes.

index

A

asparagus
  asparagus, egg and bacon
    bake E 14
  chicken, noodle and
    asparagus frittata FE 83
  tuna and asparagus crumble E 51
bacon
  asparagus, egg and bacon
    bake E 14
  cheesy chicken, tomato and
    bacon rigatoni E 75
  creamy chicken, bacon
    and corn chowder E 73
  creamy potato and bacon
    bake E 46
  egg and bacon pie E 106
  mashed potato and bacon
    bake E 44
  potato, bacon and blue
    cheese bake E 41
beef
  baked meatballs E 96
  beef ragu cannelloni 108
  beef stew with chive
    dumplings E 95
  creamy bolognese pasta
    bake E 22
  pastitsio E 18
  rich beef mince pie 102
  sausage risotto E 107
  sweet and sour meatballs E 111
  tomato, beef and pea lasagne 12
broccoli
  broccoli and cheese penne with
    garlic and lemon crumbs EV 17
  cauliflower and broccoli
    gratin EV 36

C

cannelloni
  beef ragu 108
  pumpkin, spinach and
    ricotta V 15
carbonara gnocchi bake E 5
casserole, vegie, with chive
  dumplings EV 30
cassoulet
  chicken, sausage
    and bean E 69
  pork sausage E 91
cauliflower
  cauliflower and broccoli
    gratin EV 36
  chicken biryani with cauliflower
    and peas E 86

cheese, see also fetta
  broccoli and cheese penne with
    garlic and lemon crumbs EV 17
  cheese and vegetable polenta
    bake EV 31
  cheesy chicken, tomato
    and bacon rigatoni E 75
  classic macaroni cheese EV 20
  potato, bacon and blue
    cheese bake E 41
  pumpkin, spinach and ricotta
    cannelloni V 15
chicken
  cheesy chicken, tomato and
    bacon rigatoni E 75
  chicken and broad bean
    rigatoni bake E 6
  chicken and eggplant
    parmigiana E 71
  chicken and sweet corn
    bake FE 70
  chicken biryani with
    cauliflower and peas E 86
  chicken cacciatore with gremolata
    and parmesan topping E 76
  chicken, noodle and asparagus
    frittata FE 83
  chicken penne carbonara with
    crispy crumbs E 82
  chicken, sausage and bean
    cassoulet E 69
  chicken stroganoff with potato
    topping E 85
  chicken, zucchini and
    mushroom lasagne 79
  creamy chicken, bacon and
    corn chowder E 73
  mexican chicken tortilla bake 74
  red curry chicken risotto E 72
  red wine and rosemary chicken
    with polenta crust E 89
  spicy chicken and ratatouille
    pilaf E 80
chickpea and chorizo stew E 101
chorizo and chickpea stew E 101
chowder, creamy chicken, bacon
  and corn E 73
classic macaroni cheese EV 20
corn
  chicken and sweet corn
    bake FE 70
  creamy chicken, bacon and
    corn chowder E 73
  tuna and corn bake E 67
creamed spinach E 92
creamy bolognese pasta bake E 22
creamy fish and potato bake E 64

crumble oat topping E 51
curried lentil pies EV 29

E

egg and bacon pie E 106
eggplant
  chicken and eggplant
    parmigiana E 71
  eggplant parmigiana EV 25
  lamb and eggplant pot pies
    with fetta crust E 112

F

fennel and leek gratin EV 37
fetta, see also cheese
  lamb and eggplant pot pies
    with fetta crust E 112
  prawns and fetta with crispy
    fillo 56
  pumpkin, pea and fetta
    risotto EV 32
fish, see also seafood
  creamy fish and potato bake E 64
  jansson's temptation E 55
  provençale E 59
  salmon and zucchini lasagne 52
  salmon bread and butter
    pudding E 62
  salmon, potato and rocket
    cake E 54
  salmon, silver beet and rice pie 65
  sardine, potato and lemon
    bake E 63
  smoked haddock potato
    bake E 60
  spicy sardine and spaghetti
    bake FE 57
  spicy tuna pasta bake E 66
  tuna and asparagus crumble E 51
  tuna and corn bake E 67
frittata
  chicken, noodle and
    asparagus FE 83
  potato EV 45
  rocket pesto and spaghetti EV 9

G

gnocchi
  carbonara gnocchi bake E 5
  potato gnocchi with three-cheese
    sauce EV 42
  spinach and kumara EV 26
goulash, veal, with parsley
  dumplings E 105

118

AWW COOKBOOKS ALL RECIPES TRIPLE TESTED®

TRIPLE TESTED · FOR YOUR SUCCESS EVERY TIME

BEST SELLERS

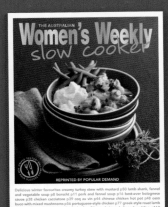

THE AUSTRALIAN **Women's Weekly** slow cooker

REPRINTED BY POPULAR DEMAND

Delicious winter favourites creamy turkey stew with mustard p50 lamb shank, fennel and vegetable soup p8 borscht p11 pork and fennel soup p16 best-ever bolognese sauce p38 chicken cacciatore p39 coq au vin p44 chinese chicken hot pot p40 osso buco with mixed mushrooms p56 portuguese-style chicken p77 greek-style roast lamb with potatoes p81 red curry lamb shanks p84 mandarin and almond pudding p112

COLLECTORS' COOKBOOK

Women's Weekly CHILDREN'S **BIRTHDAY CAKE** BOOK

VINTAGE EDITION

AUSTRALIA'S *MOST FAMOUS* CHILDREN'S CAKE BOOK

NEW COOKBOOKS

THE AUSTRALIAN **Women's Weekly** Greek cooking

Enjoy the flavours of Greece with grilled lemon chicken p80 greek salad p67 deep-fried baby calamari p28 herbed fetta cheese p12 taramasalata p9 viordala p17 eggplant fritters p24 spanakopita p36 salt cod and potato pie p56 octopus in red wine p59 rabbit stifado p64 moussaka p76 roast leg of lamb p83 pastitsio p84 stuffed eggplant p87 goat and capsicum stew p90 halva p94 baklava p102 cherry spoon sweet p110

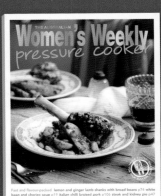

THE AUSTRALIAN **Women's Weekly** pressure cooker

Fast and flavour-packed lemon and ginger lamb shanks with broad beans p74 white bean and chorizo soup p11 italian chilli braised pork p106 steak and kidney pie p47 maple syrup and date puddings p108 chinese chicken p42 chicken with capsicum p36 pea, ham and broad bean soup p27 herb and mustard lamb leg p84 lamb and macadamia curry p80 coq au vin p28 spicy lamb in tomato and spinach sauce p73

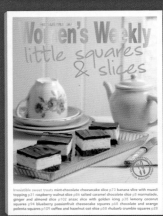

THE AUSTRALIAN **Women's Weekly** little squares & slices

Irresistible sweet treats mint-chocolate cheesecake slice p73 banana slice with muesli topping p31 raspberry walnut slice p86 salted caramel chocolate slice p10 marmalade, ginger and almond slice p102 anzac slice p38 lemony coconut squares p94 blueberry passionfruit cheesecake squares p66 chocolate and orange polenta squares p109 coffee and hazelnut oat slice p58 rhubarb crumble squares p28

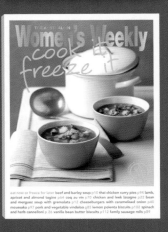

THE AUSTRALIAN **Women's Weekly** cook freeze it

eat now or freeze for later beef and barley soup p10 thai chicken curry pies p94 lamb, apricot and almond tagine p66 coq au vin p70 chicken and leek lasagne p22 bean and merguez soup with gremolata p12 cheeseburgers with caramelised onion p40 moussaka p97 pork and vegetable vindaloo p85 lemon polenta biscuits p102 spinach and herb cannelloni p26 vanilla bean butter biscuits p112 family sausage rolls p58

The extensive range of Australian Women's Weekly cookbooks are on sale at selected newsagents and supermarkets or online at
www.acpbooks.com.au

Published in 2011 by ACP Books, Sydney

ACP Books are published by ACP Magazines a division of Nine Entertainment Co.

ACP BOOKS

General manager Christine Whiston
Associate publisher Seymour Cohen
Editor-in-chief Susan Tomnay
Creative director & designer Hieu Chi Nguyen
Art director Hannah Blackmore
Senior editor Kirsty McKenzie
Food director Pamela Clark
Senior food editor Rebecca Squadrito
Sales & rights director Brian Cearnes
Marketing manager Bridget Cody
Senior business analyst Rebecca Varela
Operations manager David Scotto
Production manager Victoria Jefferys
Circulation manager Sarah Lloyd
Circulation analyst Nicole Pearson
Published by ACP Books, a division of ACP Magazines Ltd, 54 Park St, Sydney; GPO Box 4088, Sydney, NSW 2001. phone (02) 9282 8618; fax (02) 9267 9438. acpbooks@acpmagazines.com.au; www.acpbooks.com.au

Printed by Toppan Printing Co, China.

Australia Distributed by Network Services, phone +61 2 9282 8777; fax +61 2 9264 3278; networkweb@networkservicescompany.com.au
New Zealand Distributed by Netlink Distribution Company, phone (9) 366 9966; ask@ndc.co.nz
South Africa Distributed by PSD Promotions, phone (27 11) 392 6065/6/7; fax (27 11) 392 6079/80; orders@psdprom.co.za

Title: Bakes & gratins / food director Pamela Clark
ISBN: 978-1-74245-069-8 (pbk.)
Notes: Includes index.
Subjects: Baking. Roasting (Cooking)
Other authors/contributors: Clark, Pamela
Dewey number: 641.71

Recipe development Nicole Dicker, Sharon Kennedy, Lucy Nunes, Rebecca Squadrito
Nutritional information Rebecca Squadrito

Photographer Julie Crespel
Stylist Kate Brown
Food preparation Emma McCaskill
Cover Cheesy chicken, tomato and bacon rigatoni, page 75

To order books
phone 136 116 (within Australia) or
order online at www.acpbooks.com.au
Send recipe enquiries to:
recipeenquiries@acpmagazines.com.au